The Joy of Teaching

of

Teaching

A Devotional for Teachers

Preventing and overcoming burnout in the profession that you love

SHARRON MARCUS

Cocoon to Wings
PUBLISHING

THE JOY OF TEACHING

Copyright © 2024 Sharron Marcus

Printed in the United States of America

ISBN: 978-1-953497-99-4 (Paperback)

Library of Congress Control Number: 2024904937

Published by Cocoon to Wings Publishing

7810 Gall Blvd., #311

Zephyrhills, FL 33541

www.CocoontoWingsBooks.com

(813) 906-WING (9464)

Cover Design by ETP Creative

The Joy of of Teaching

A Devotional for Teachers

Preventing and overcoming burnout in the profession that you love

Cocoon to Wings
PUBLISHING

Dedication

To Alton – Thank you for the dedication and support
along my journey in education.

Introduction

THE CALLING TO TEACH IS a high calling from God. Teaching is by far one of the most rewarding yet challenging professions. You will not fulfill this calling with the same passion and joy you began with if you are not intentional about spending time with God. To be an effective teacher and bear fruit in this profession, you must stay connected to the vine (John 15:5). Apart from Him, you can do nothing. This devotional is designed to help teachers transition from merely surviving to thriving in the profession they hold dear. If you commit to partnering with God, He will give you the strength and wisdom to ensure that your impact transcends your classroom.

I must also include a word of caution as you embark on this new semester or school year. Teaching comes with huge accountability and responsibility from the Lord. Children are precious in the eyes of God. He specially created and designed every child who will set foot in your classroom. Jesus said it would be better that a millstone be hung around a person's neck, and they drown in the depths of the sea than for them to offend one of these little ones. (Luke 17:1-2). As an educator, you must heed God's Word and approach your role with the utmost seriousness recognizing your profound impact on the lives entrusted to our care.

At a time when many educators are walking away, remember that you work for the "Most High" and it is He who has called you to the profession for such a time as this. Prioritizing God, through daily devotions to Him, will provide the strength needed for days ahead. By aligning with God, you will realize your dream of positively impacting your students and cultivate greater happiness, patience, and joy. Consider consecrating a fast at the beginning of each semester to seek God's face. Resist the temptation to abandon your calling; stay the course, trusting that God will reward your obedience and dedication.

This 90-day devotional includes scriptures, words of encouragement, and stories from amazing educators I have encountered in my 32 years as an educator. The prayers at the end of each day are suggestions for your conversation with God. Remember to add your own words and do not forget that it is a conversation, so take time to listen. Peace and blessings on a great semester!

Daily Confessions

1. I am the righteousness of God in Christ Jesus.
2. I am a son/daughter of The "Most High" God.
3. I am on divine assignment for The Kingdom of God.
4. I set the tone and the atmosphere for my classroom/school.
5. I am a model of God's love in my classroom.
6. Every child in my classroom was purposely placed there by God Himself.
7. God is on my side and has given me the victory in my classroom this year.
8. I operate from a position of divine authority, abundance, and power in my classroom.
9. I am more than a conqueror in Christ Jesus.
10. I submit to God's divine authority to help me, and my students have a successful school year.

Beginning of the New Year/Semester – Without Him, You Can Do Nothing

I am the vine; you are the branches. He that abides in Me, and I in him, bears much fruit; for without Me you can do nothing. John 15:5 (NKJV)

THE BEGINNING OF THE YEAR or semester is the most crucial time of the school year. During the days of planning before students arrive, ask God to help you create an environment that is welcoming and inviting for His children. Before you move one desk or put up one poster, dedicate your classroom to God and invite Him into your space. Carve out some time to meet privately with Him, allowing your classroom to become a sanctuary. Consider getting on your knees in the middle of the room as an act of humility and ask The Creator to bless your school and give you inspiration, direction, wisdom, and guidance for the year. God has divinely created every child that will cross your path. I recommend writing the names of each student in a journal and regularly praying for them and their families. The effectual fervent prayers of the righteous availeth much (James 5:16).

Abba,

I acknowledge that You are the true and living God of the universe. I thank You for choosing me to work with Your children. Thank You for this school year and this classroom. I dedicate this space to You. I ask that You go before me this school year and make the crooked places straight. I know that apart from You, I can do nothing. I consecrate myself for Your service this year. I take authority over my classroom as I subject myself to Your divine authority. Give me wisdom and direction for the semester ahead. Give me the heart to love each of Your children and may I learn as much from them as they will learn from me.

In Jesus' Name
Amen

Day 1 - Ambassador for Christ

Now then we are ambassadors for Christ, as though God did beseech you by us: we pray you on Christ's stead, be ye reconciled to God. 2 Corinthians 5:20

AS A TEACHER AND FOLLOWER of Christ, you are not just an educator but an ambassador for The Kingdom of Heaven. You are a living model of God's love within your classroom. An ambassador is a designated official acting as a representative of a nation. You have been chosen and approved by The Kingdom of God to be His representative in your classroom, your school, and your district. You set the atmosphere and the tone for your classroom on the first day. The success of the entire school year hinges upon the foundation laid during the first days of school. By establishing clear expectations, building positive relationships, and fostering a structured learning environment, you set the tone for the entire year. Your approach as an ambassador for Christ during the first weeks of school will profoundly impact your students and the school community. Put in the extra hours at the beginning of the semester to write and communicate clear rituals and routines for each aspect of the classroom and the school day. Take the time to call parents and build positive relationships from the onset. While this may be a big task, remember you are not alone. You have The Almighty God and the forces of heaven working on your behalf. Never forget that God has chosen you and is the one who is working through you for the work that was chosen for you before the foundation of the world. Remember, The Almighty God is on your side (Psalm 118:6).

Abba,

As I start this first day of a new school year/semester, I thank You for new beginnings. Thank You for choosing me to work with Your children. Thank You that You have assigned me to the students, parents, and colleagues at this school. Help me to always remember that I am an ambassador for You. I represent The Kingdom of Heaven in my classroom, school, and district. Before You formed me in my mother's womb, You knew me and chose me for this appointed task. As my students enter my classroom today, help me to know that You made each one and You have selected each one to sit under my teaching this school year. I commit this new school year to You and ask that You go before me to make the crooked places straight. Give me the divine wisdom and guidance I need for a successful first day of school. I pray for each student under my care today. I pray that they will see You in me.

In Jesus' Name
Amen

Day 2 – Life and Death

Death and life are in the power of the tongue: And they that love it shall eat the fruit thereof. Proverbs 18:21

YOU HAVE BEEN CREATED IN the likeness of God, and just as the Almighty spoke words to shape the world, your words also carry creative power. This year, commit to refrain from speaking negatively about your students, parents, school, or community. Be intentional about making this a great semester by committing to seeing and speaking the good. Remember to always speak positively about the people God has called you to serve. The power of your words can shape your reality, so focus on speaking words of encouragement and affirmation. Even in private conversations, strive to speak only words that build up and inspire those around you. By doing so, you can create a more positive and uplifting environment for all. In a world comfortable with criticizing children and labeling them as "bad," remember the biblical warning that you will give an account for every idle word (Matthew 12:36). When reflecting on some of the most inspiring educators I have had the privilege of working with, Ms. Willie Mae Chaney stands out. Ms. Chaney mastered the art of using her words to speak life. Each morning, she consistently greet-

2

ed her special needs students with a smile and a personalized word of encouragement. She made each student feel seen and valued. Her encouraging words created a positive and uplifting atmosphere within her classroom and the entire school. These positive, faith-filled words motivated and empowered students to excel academically. Her positive attitude was contagious, impacting other educators and the entire school community. Like Ms. Chaney, your words will impact the environment positively or negatively. You have the power to speak life or death over your classroom and school environment. Choose to speak life.

Abba,

Thank You that You have created me in Your image and that my words have creative power. Help me to see the best in others just like You see the best in me. Thank You that while we were yet sinners, You sent Your Son to die on the cross for our sins. Set a guard over the door of my mouth and let no unwholesome words come out of my mouth about Your children, their parents, the leaders of this school, or anyone in the community. Help me to use my words to speak life. I come against any negative thoughts about others that don't line up with Your Words. I choose to think about things that are of good report about the people You have assigned me to serve. Help me to always remember that I will give an account of every idle word that comes out of my mouth. You are The Potter, and I am the clay. Continue to shape me and mold me into the image of Your Son, Jesus.
In Jesus'
Amen

Day 3 Called to Serve

But he that is greatest among you shall be your servant.
Matthew 23:11

THE CALLING OF EDUCATORS IS to teach as well as to serve. A servant is someone dedicated to performing duties for others. Just like servers in a restaurant attend to the needs of customers, we are called to serve our students, their parents, colleagues, and administrators. This is the opposite of our present culture, which often prioritizes being served. Embrace the teachings of Jesus, who emphasized that true greatness comes through service. Jesus came to the world not to be served but to serve. He modeled this behavior in all His actions, healing the sick, restoring sight to the blind, and washing the feet of his disciples (including Judas). As a Kingdom educator, you must have a servant's heart. During class, when students are working independently or collaboratively, teachers with a heart to serve are up and walking around the room, looking for ways to serve and provide feedback to enhance the learning process. When opportunities arise to contribute to committees or tasks within the school community, view those as opportunities to fulfill your calling. Your call to serve does not end when the last bell sounds, reach out to children past the school day by attending their sporting events and extracurricular activities. Teaching, at its core, is an act of service. By putting the needs of others first, you can create an environment where students not only learn academically but grow into productive citizens who understand the power of serving others. As Christians, we are God's hands, feet, and mouthpiece in our classrooms, schools, and communities. Jesus taught us that to be great, we must serve others.

Abba,

Thank You for Jesus' example. Thank You that He humbled Himself and served others. I submit to Your divine authority in my life. I humble myself under Your mighty hand. I submit myself to the leaders of this school and this community. I surrender myself for Your use and Your purposes in my classroom and my school. Show me how to humbly serve others without complaining. Use my hands, my feet, and my mouth for Your service. Show me which tasks and assignments are for me to handle at my school, in my department, or at my grade level. Help me to have the mind of Christ and look for ways to serve, expecting nothing in return. You are my Rewarder and The Lifter of my head.

In Jesus' Name
Amen

Day 4 Be Still and Know

Be still, and know that I am God: I will be exalted among the nations, I will be exalted in the earth! Psalm 46:10 (NKJV)

YOU MUST TAKE TIME EACH day to "be still and know" that God sits on the throne. In those moments, let the peace of God fill your heart, bringing reassurance, strength, and a renewed sense of purpose. Allow your quiet time with God to serve as your life source, providing the necessary fuel for your journey. Neglecting this vital time of connection with your Creator is a risk you cannot afford to take. As a teacher, you will often bear the weight of concerns for your students, their families, and of situations that appear beyond your ability to change. The challenges of life, and especially the profession, can seem overwhelming; therefore, disciplining yourself to consistently spend time with God is imperative. God invites you to cast your cares upon Him, extending rest to all who are weary and burdened. An active prayer life serves as the remedy, nurturing the soul and sustaining the passion needed to sustain you. Regular prayer with God not only provides a clearer perspective on the magnitude of His power but also serves as a reminder that He is in complete control. Your quiet moments with God offer a safe place to unload the burdens of teaching, family demands, and other life stressors. By starting each day fresh and rested, having spent time in quiet communion with God, you position yourself to better serve others. God becomes a refreshing well of living water, quenching the daily thirst created by the demands of your life as a teacher. If you make the Lord your dwelling place, He will sustain you in this profession.

Abba,

I take the time to "be still and know" that You are God. Thank You for the invitation to come unto You and cast my cares upon You. I thank You for my job and the opportunity to influence Your children each day. I come humbly to enjoy the refreshing presence of Your Spirit. In Your presence, there is fullness of joy, and at Your right hand, there are pleasures forever more. I come boldly to Your throne to receive the grace and mercy that I need. I confess that I cannot do this job without You. I declare my dependency on You. Thank You for being an ever-present help for me. I pray for my students and their families.

In Jesus' Name
Amen

Day 5 Embracing Challenges

My brethren, count it all joy, when you fall into various trials,
knowing that the testing of your faith produces patience.
But let patience have its perfect work, that you may be perfect
and complete, wanting nothing. James 1:2 (NKJV)

AS AN EDUCATOR, YOU WILL unavoidably encounter various challenges throughout your career. In today's scripture, you are admonished not to see these challenges as hindrances but to consider them "joy." Each trial, whether big or small, contributes to developing your teaching skills and nurturing your faith so that you will be complete. Jesus warned that conflicts are inevitable in this world (John 16:33). Spending time with God in the secret place will strengthen you emotionally and help you to see the trials that you face from His perspective. As you face conflict each day, it is so important that you remain calm and seek solutions. Make up your mind that when things do not go as planned, you will remain joyful. Stay flexible and be prepared to pivot when needed. When technology issues arise that disrupt your planned lesson, find ways to turn the unexpected challenge into an opportunity for student engagement. One effective teacher who loved children's stories was always ready with a favorite read-aloud book anytime there were technological interruptions or when she felt her students needed a brain break. Keep a contingency plan that requires few resources to continue learning when interruptions arise. You must learn to quickly adjust to trials, knowing that God is causing all things to work together for good. Make the decision early on that when faced with an angry parent, you will remain calm. Like a good student, strive to pass the small daily tests of life by choosing the path of godliness and peace. When problems arise, students will watch your reaction in the face of these challenges. They learn not just about the subject matter but also about resilience, adaptability, and the importance of maintaining a positive attitude in the face of unexpected obstacles.

Abba,

Thank You for another day filled with new grace and mercy. Father, today, I take up my cross, deny myself, and follow You. Give me wisdom in my earthly relationships and interactions with others. As much as possible, I will do my best to walk peaceably with my fellow man. I thank You for Jesus' example of overcoming persecution and opposition. I know that You are causing every situation to work together for my good. I put on Your whole armor, knowing that You have equipped me to pass every test. I deny myself and cast away my need to be right or have the final word. I submit myself to You today, and I trust what You are doing in my life.

In Jesus' Name
Amen

Day 6 A New Thing

Remember ye not the former things, neither consider the things of old. Behold, I will do a new thing; now it shall spring forth; shall ye not know it? I will even make a way in the wilderness and rivers in the desert. Isaiah 43:18-19

EVERY DAY GOD LOADS YOU with new benefits (Psalm 68:19) and graciously forgives your past. Forget about the previous school year/semester and things that may have happened in the past. As you familiarize yourself with your students, resist the temptation to delve into their past academic records or engage in discussions with fellow teachers about their history. Refrain from dwelling on the failures of past students, as everyone deserves the same fresh start that God grants you each day. Upon learning that she would have an infamous set of twins in her class, Amber Marcus immediately began thinking negative thoughts. She remembered the stories of their behavior in the past and even witnessed some of these behaviors firsthand. Realizing that seeing their names on her roster filled her with anxiety about the new year, Amber turned to prayer and asked God for guidance, humility, and an open heart toward the children. Committed to giving the twins a fresh start, she also decided to form a trusting relationship with the girls' parents. In the end, Amber formed a strong teacher-student-parent bond that not only impacted the twins' academic journey but also left a lingering impression on the school community demonstrating the power of breaking free from prejudgment. Today's scripture admonishes you to "forget the former things". As a child of God, you are the "salt of the Earth" and you are the "light of the world" (Matthew 5:13-14). Do not lose your flavor or dim your light by judging others on their past mistakes.

Abba,

Thank You for a new day and a new school year. I praise You that You know all, and You see all. You are the omnipresent God, and nothing is hidden from Your presence. Thank You that You have not condemned me according to my sins. Thank You that You daily load me with benefits and do not hold my past against me. As I begin this new school year, help me to guard my thoughts and my heart against remembering the pasts of others. Help me to model Your love in my classroom and give every student the grace and mercy that You have shown me. Help me to walk in love and forgiveness in every interaction. Guard me from every conversation that would influence me negatively about each student every day.

In Jesus' Name,
Amen

Day 7 Fully Equipped

According as His divine power has given to us all things that pertain to life and godliness, through the knowledge of Him that hath called us to glory and virtue: 2 Peter 1:3

EDUCATION IS A CONSTANTLY CHANGING profession. There is always a new program, new strategy, or a perceived better way to do things. You must not be easily moved or frustrated by change. Because you are fully equipped by the indwelling Holy Spirit for the assignment as an educator, you can embrace change. It does not matter if you are in a new subject, teaching a new grade level, or if education was not your first career choice. The Creator of the universe is the author of it all. Regardless of what you are teaching, He created it. Ms. Kylie Garrard stands as a remarkable success story in the field of education. Embarking on teaching as a second career, she faced challenges during the initial change to her career path. Confronting the early waves of discouragement, Kylie persevered through the difficulties and emerged victorious. Her journey saw her not only overcoming obstacles but flourishing to the point of being recognized as Teacher of the Year and eventually achieving the status of Master Teacher. Much like Ms. Garrard, your passion for teaching, dedication to your students, and openness to learning are your greatest assets. As you navigate your professional journey, it is essential to recognize that with the Holy Spirit within you, you possess everything necessary to learn, teach, and implement lessons effectively. You are fully equipped! In your professional journey, seek God's wisdom and guidance. Acknowledge your dependence on Him, and as you commit your ways to Him, He promises to make your path straight (Proverbs 3:6). Embrace the changes that come, knowing that with His divine power, you can navigate and excel in every aspect of your educational journey.

Abba,

Thank You that the Earth is Yours and everything in it. This school and the children all belong to You. I belong to You. As I am set to teach this content, I understand that You are the author of it all. I cast aside any feelings of anxiety and inferiority. Give me the divine wisdom that I need today to teach Your children. May Your Holy Spirit living on the inside of me give me revelation, knowledge, and the understanding that I need. Use me as Your instrument to teach Your children. Thank You that You have fully equipped me by giving me everything I need as it pertains to life and godliness.

In Jesus' Name
Amen

Day 8 First Things First

---

*But seek ye first the kingdom of God and His righteousness;
and all these things shall be added unto you. Matthew 6:33*

MOST EDUCATORS SHARE A COMMON goal to serve with excellence and make a lasting difference in the lives of the children they teach. The key to achieving this goal, however, is not solely rooted in having the best lesson plans, curriculum documents, or instructional strategies. Instead, it begins with prioritizing and seeking God first, acknowledging His rightful place in your life. To seek first The Kingdom, as commanded in this verse, means to carve out time at the start of each day to acknowledge God, read His Word, pray, and present yourself to Him. Dedicate your mornings to seeking wisdom and guidance for the day ahead, and in the evening, reflect on your experiences, expressing gratitude and seeking strength in areas where challenges arise. This may require you to shift your routine and make a commitment to getting to bed earlier and waking up earlier, but the reward will be worth it. Reflecting on the wisdom imparted to Joshua, God encouraged Joshua not to let the book of the law depart from his mouth but to meditate on it day and night, promising that then he would make his way prosperous (Joshua 1:8). God understands our needs and has instructed us to prioritize seeking Him, assuring that He will provide for all our other needs. It is time to trust God's Word and recognize that becoming an effective teacher is inseparable from our connection with God. Without Him, our efforts lack lasting significance, and it is through acknowledging and aligning ourselves with His guidance that we truly thrive in our roles as educators.

Abba,

Thank You for this day. Thank You for my career as an educator. I acknowledge that I need your divine help and wisdom to be the teacher that You have called me to be. I come today to seek first Your Kingdom. I prioritize You in my life. I welcome Your abiding Spirit, knowing that apart from You, I can do nothing. You are my source and my sustainer. You know all things, and You know what I need. I present my body to You today as a living sacrifice. I submit my day, my life, and my career to You. It all belongs to You. I trust Your Word that says that You will add all of the things that I need when I seek You first.

In Jesus' Name,
Amen

Day 9 Called to Encourage

Let no corrupt communication proceed out of your mouth, but that which to the use of edifying that it may minister grace unto the hearers. Ephesians 4:29

YOU ARE CALLED TO BE an encourager! Your words have the power to edify and bring grace. Your words also have the power to dishonor, creating permanent damage. Yet, like sweet honeycomb, choose to use your words to encourage others, including children, administrators, and coworkers. Your words have the power to build or to destroy. A close friend and administrator, Dr. Renee' Mays often reminded educators to "taste their words" before speaking. She encouraged them to consider the potential "flavor" of their words, whether they are sweet and uplifting or bitter and hurtful. Her words have stuck with me over the years as a call to understand the power of my words. Consider the weight that your words carry. Let the words that you speak affirm and validate children. In the moments of teaching, guiding, and interacting with your students, be conscious of the responsibility to speak words that uplift, inspire, and encourage. Jesus admonished believers that they will give an account of every idle word spoken (Matthew 12:36). It is important to make positive phone calls to parents instead of limiting calls to only reporting bad news. When you talk to parents, remember to start every conversation with something good. Reach out to parents to build trusting relationships and to let them know you look forward to and enjoy teaching their children. Find ways to phrase your written and verbal feedback to students in a positive way. Never forget that you are teaching future doctors, lawyers, teachers, and preachers too. Do not discount what God can do in the lives of the children you teach. Your words have the power to make a lasting impression - speak life!

Abba,

Thank You for life, health, and strength. Thank You for the power of my words to build and encourage. I ask that You put a guard over the door of my mouth and let no corrupt communication come out of my mouth but that which is good. Help me to always respond to others in love. Give me the wisdom to use my words to build up children, my administrators, and my coworkers. Use my voice to affirm Your children and their families. Help me always see the good and to use my words to edify others. Help me to always remember that I am a model of Your love in my classroom. Let my speech be full of grace and seasoned with salt. Give me the wisdom and self-control to know how to respond appropriately in every situation.

In Jesus' Name
Amen

Day 10 Seeking Wisdom

If any of you lacks wisdom, let him ask of God who gives to all men liberally and without reproach, and it will be given to him. James 1:5 (NKJV)

THE PROMISE OF RECEIVING WISDOM without criticism is a reassuring reminder that, when faced with uncertainties or dilemmas, we have the privilege of seeking divine wisdom through prayer. Wisdom is more than having knowledge. Wisdom is knowing the correct actions to take at the correct time based on knowledge. Wisdom is knowing what a child needs and when the child needs it. Wisdom is knowing when to follow the lesson plan and when to use the teachable moments to impart life lessons. Wisdom is knowing when to talk and when to keep quiet. Wisdom is knowing when to say yes and when to say no to requests to serve. Wisdom is knowing God's divine purposes and His will for Your life. The Bible teaches that wisdom and understanding are better than silver, gold, and earthly riches (Proverbs 16:16). You cannot be an effective teacher without God and His wisdom. Coach Minnie Harper, a distinguished educator with over 50 years of service, is a testament to the profound impact of wisdom in the realm of teaching. She shares a touching story of creating an environment where a student felt secure enough to disclose an abusive relationship. In this crucial moment, God endowed Coach Harper with the wisdom necessary to navigate the delicate situation. With discernment and care, she ensured the immediate safety and well-being of the student. Coach Harper's story stands as a powerful example of how wisdom, guided by compassion, can make a significant difference in the lives of students, even in the face of challenging circumstances. King Solomon is a biblical example of the need for wisdom. He could have asked God for anything, but he knew that he would need wisdom to lead God's people (1 Kings 3:9). The Bible tells us that King Solomon's request pleased God. Like King Solomon, we can pray and ask God and He will give wisdom to us liberally without reservation. That's good news!

Abba,

Thank You for another day's journey. Thank You that You are the all-knowing and all-seeing God. I thank You for the opportunity to teach Your children and I confess that I cannot teach them without Your help. You know exactly what each of them needs. I come humbly asking You for wisdom to teach them collectively and individually. I ask You for wisdom to know when to speak and when it is best for me to just keep quiet. Guide my tongue in every conversation that I have with students, parents, and coworkers. I need Your wisdom and I thank You that You have said that all I need to do is ask and that You will impart wisdom to me without reservation. I thank You for the wisdom that You are providing to me today.

In Jesus' Name,
Amen

Day 11 Like Jesus

For whom He foreknew, He also predestined to be conformed to the image of His Son, that He might be the firstborn among many brethren. Romans 8:29 (NKJV)

EVERY CHILD THAT SITS IN your classroom has a purpose and a potential that you are helping to nurture and develop. The future of the world is sitting in your classroom; this is not just a cliche. You could be nurturing the skills and dreams of the next president, ground-breaking scientist, or industry trailblazer. Every student has the potential to make a significant impact on society, and it is your duty as a teacher to help them realize their potential. It is a beautiful thing to be entrusted with such an important role in shaping the future. Take heart in the fact that God is working on you and your students. According to today's scripture, you are going through a metamorphosis that will transform you into the likeness of Jesus. The same is true for every person and every child that sits in your classroom. The beautiful part is God has selected you to help tend to the early stages of your students' development. You have a major impact on them, and they probably go home each night repeating something you have said. Many teachers do not realize the impact they have on young lives. As a teacher, you play an important role in the overall growth and development of your students, nurturing their talents, skills, and character. Embrace your role in the development of the next generation, and trust in the transformative process, both in your own life and the life of your students. Keep up the great work and continue to improve and grow in the profession!

Abba,

Thank You for a new day and a new opportunity to shape the future of the world. I submit my life and this day to Your divine hand and authority. Thank You that You have a purpose and a plan for my life. I trust what You are doing in me and through me. Thank You for the opportunity to model Your love and care in my classroom. Help me to always remember that You love my students and that You have selected me to teach them. You have not made any mistakes and You have a plan and purpose for each of them. Thank You for including me in Your plans for their lives. Go before me today to make the crooked places straight. I commit this day to Your plans and Your purposes. May Your will be done in my classroom and my life today.

In Jesus' Name,
Amen

Day 12 Dominion & Authority

Then He called his twelve disciples together and gave them power and authority... Luke 9:1

As a follower of Jesus Christ, you have been given the power and authority to make a positive impact on your students. This authority is fostered in the secret place of His presence, so it is essential to spend time with Him to walk in your Kingdom authority. This authority looks like confidence and communicates high expectations commanding attention and respect from those around you. From her early beginnings as an educator at Staley Middle School, Victoria Harris was a born teacher and esteemed leader. She carries herself with a Godly confidence that draws respect from those in her presence. Her confident posture and gestures communicated that she was not someone to be trifled with, making her a beacon of inspiration for students and colleagues alike. With a perfect balance of firmness and fairness, your presence should similarly command attention and inspire confidence in your skills. Your body language and verbal and non-verbal communication should exemplify the dominion and authority that you possess. Your students and others will recognize and respect this God-given authority. It is common for students to intuitively determine the level of respect they have for teachers based on the perceived authority the teacher conveys. As you walk in this authority, strive to arrive to work early regularly to set the tone and command the atmosphere and environment. As a follower of Jesus, you can tap into a unique source of authority and confidence, and by doing so, positively impact the lives of students. Boldly decree the things you would like to see happen (Job 22:28) in your classroom. In every interaction, strive to be a beacon of kindness, compassion, and encouragement. Recognize the divine purpose that brought you to the field of education and let that purpose guide your actions. Walk in the power and authority that Jesus has bestowed upon you.

Abba,

I praise You that You are the Most High God and that there is none stronger or higher. I thank You for the secret place of Your presence. I thank You that this is the place where You strengthen me and show me my authority in You. I thank You for the dominion and authority that You have given me as Your child. I understand that I set the tone and the atmosphere in my classroom. I declare and decree peace and order to this day. I take authority over every student that will enter this classroom. I walk in the confidence and the authority that You have given to me as Your child. I declare safety, peace, and order to this day. I bind and rebuke every attempt of the enemy to hinder my efforts. I bless this day and every child that enters my classroom. May Your light and authority shine through me today.

In Jesus' Name
Amen

Day 13 Labor for the Lord

Except the LORD build the house, They labour in vain that build it: Except the LORD keep the city, The watchman waketh but in vain. Psalm 127:1

LIKE AN ARCHITECT WHO PLANS and designs a building, as a teacher, you are tasked with constructing a learning environment that lays a foundation for success beyond the classroom. According to today's scripture, that foundation must include God. Without His presence and guidance, all human efforts are fruitless. Imagine building an entire house in vain or staying up all night to guard a city in vain. The message is clear: unless God builds your classroom, you are building in vain. Unless God watches over your classroom and school, the security plans are in vain. By seeking His guidance, you can trust that He will lead you in the right direction and provide you with the wisdom and strength needed for effectiveness. It does not matter how good the lesson plans are and how good the school's safety plans are, God is in complete control of everything. The Earth is the LORD's and everything in it. Allow God to build your classroom by surrendering it to Him. It all belongs to Him anyway. Although He has given humanity free will, surrendering your plans to His sovereign will is an act of acknowledging His authority. It is easy to get caught up in school goals and improvement plans yet forget about the bigger picture. Proverbs 21:31 (NIV) states that the horse is made ready for the day of battle, but victory rests with the LORD. In the same way, we can prepare and plan, but we must trust in God's protection and sovereignty over everything. By surrendering our plans to His will, we can find peace and confidence in His authority over our lives.

Abba,

I thank You that You are the Most High God. I declare that heaven is Your throne and Earth is Your footstool. You are the final authority on Earth, and You are in complete control. You open doors that no man can shut. I surrender my life to You. I declare that my classroom and my school belong to You and that this is holy ground. Show me how to allow You to rule and reign through me. Give me eyes to see and ears to hear the voice of Your Spirit. Thank You that You have given Your angels charge over me. I ask You to build and watch over my classroom and this school so I do not labor in vain. I pray for Your divine protection over every student in my classroom and this school. I thank You that Your favor surrounds me like a shield. May Your will be done in my life and this school.

In Jesus' Name
Amen

Day 14 Chosen by God

Ye are my witnesses, saith the LORD, and my servant whom I have chosen... Isaiah 43:10

IT IS NOT A COINCIDENCE that you find yourself in the role of an educator. Whether you serve in elementary, middle, or high school, you have been chosen by God for this assignment. The scriptures affirm that all your days were preordained before even one of them came into existence (Psalm 139:16 NIV). Your placement in your specific school within your district is not random but it is a divine appointment and assignment orchestrated by God. Consider the story of Emily, a young teacher who, as a college freshman, fervently prayed and sensed a calling to the teaching profession. Despite encountering skepticism from family members and friends who, with good intentions, urged her to reconsider, Emily stood firm in her conviction. She believed that teaching was her calling and that she possessed the ability to positively impact the lives of students. After the first few years of teaching, her family, and friends, who once questioned her career choice, witnessed the joy that teaching brought to Emily's life and the lives she touched. Her journey stands as a testimony to the resilience of a calling and the power of prayer. Like Emily, you must not allow people or circumstances to cause you to second guess your purpose and assignment. Trust that God called you to the noble profession and is in complete control. Stay focused on the assignment and keep your mind on God. Trust that He is using you to make a difference in the lives of your students and the community. God is The Author and The Finisher of our faith (Hebrews 12:2). He has started a good work in you, and He is well able to finish it. Your students are counting on you, and the world needs more educators like you.

Abba,

Oh God, You are my God. Thank You for this day. Thank You for choosing me to work with Your children. I accept my divine assignment. I trust You and I know that You have not made any mistakes and that this day was ordained before it came to pass. Give me the wisdom and guidance I need to work with each of Your children today. Help me to walk worthy of Your divine calling on my life. I thank You for the good days and the challenging days of my job. I do not allow situations and circumstances that arise to cause me to doubt Your plans for my life. I know that You are causing everything to work for my good. I focus my mind on You, knowing that You will keep me in perfect peace.

In Jesus' Name
Amen.

Day 15 Do Not Grow Weary

---

*And let us not grow weary in well-doing, for in due season
we shall reap, if we faint not. Galatians 6:9*

THE SCRIPTURE ENCOURAGES BELIEVERS TO persevere in well-doing, even when weariness threatens to set in. In your journey
as an educator, you will inevitably face challenging days, both
professionally and personally. There will be instances where you
encounter disobedient and troubled students, as well as parents
who may not provide the support you hope for. But just as a
farmer patiently tends to the fields, you can also remain steadfast
in your commitment to education. Your due season is marked by
the success and growth of your students. The path of education
can be demanding, and there may be moments when weariness
threatens to overshadow the impact of your hard work. It is precisely during these times that the scripture encourages us to stand
firm, to continue sowing seeds of excellence with unwavering
resolve. Whether you are a new educator or have been in the
field for years, remember that your hard work matters and can
make a positive impact. A notable example is Ms. Valarie Trice,
who taught for several years before retiring due to medical reasons. Even after retiring her passion for education and her love

for children showed no signs of waning. With God's help even in retirement, she continued to tutor students and write children's books. Her unwavering commitment ensured that instead of growing weary, she continued to evolve as an educator and will leave a lasting impact on countless lives. Ask God to help you keep your passion for the profession and not grow weary. Trust in the promise that, with God's guidance, your commitment to education can evolve and leave a legacy.

Abba,

I seek first Your Kingdom today, and I know that You have promised that You will add to me the other things that I need. I trust what You are doing in my life during this season. I set my affection and attention on You. I invite You into every detail of my classroom. Help me to not grow weary in well-doing. Help me to give others the same grace and mercy that You so freely give to me each day. Forgive me for participating or listening to any gossip about others. I lift my students and their parents to You. I lift my school leaders to You. Give them wisdom as they make decisions for the school. May Your will be done in my life, in my classroom, and in this school today.

In Jesus' Name
Amen

Day 16 Humility in Christ

Let this mind be in you, which was also in Christ Jesus: Who, being in the form of God, thought it not robbery to be equal with God: but made Himself of no reputation and took upon Him the form of a servant, and was made in the likeness of men: Philippians 2:5-7

YOU HAVE AN AMAZING SAVIOR in Jesus! He was God, yet He lowered Himself, came to Earth, and subjected Himself to human authority. Take confidence in knowing that no man took His life, He laid it down (John 10:18). Today's scripture admonishes us to take on the character of Jesus. Having the mind of Christ means that you must humble yourself like Christ. Humility in the field of education is crucial for both teachers and students. It allows teachers to approach their students with empathy and understanding, and it helps students to learn with an open mind and a willingness to receive guidance and correction. When we cultivate humility in ourselves, we become more like Jesus, who demonstrated humility in all aspects of his life. It is important to maintain a humble attitude and avoid being self-centered. Focus on doing the right thing for the benefit of your students and the community. By serving and building others, you can make a positive impact and model the life of Christ. God resists the proud but gives grace to the humble (1 Peter 5:5). Mrs. Bettye Carter, a fellow teacher at Staley Middle School, was a great example of Christ in the classroom. She believed in the importance of building meaningful relationships with her students. She took the time to listen to their concerns and offered academic guidance and emotional support. Through her caring and empathic approach, she aimed to demonstrate the love of Christ in action. May we follow the example of Mrs. Bettye Carter and make a positive impact on the lives of those around us. Remember Jesus, who showed us how to live a life of humility and service.

Abba,

Thank You for a sweet Savior in Jesus. Thank You that He has preeminence in everything. Thank You for shaping me into His very image. I submit myself to Your authority and I allow Your Word to renew my mind. Thank You for the opportunity to work with Your children each day. Help me to not take it for granted. As I set out to teach Your students today, I remember that You are my strength, and You are my source. I take on the mind of Christ today. Just like he lowered Himself and became a man, I lower myself as Your servant today. I esteem others as higher and better than myself. Like Jesus, I make myself of no reputation. I set out to be the best teacher I can be for You and not for recognition from people. I thank You that You are my Rewarder, and I am Your representative in my classroom and in this school today.

In Jesus' Name
Amen

Day 17 God is The Rewarder

Take heed that ye do not your alms before men, to be seen of them: otherwise, ye have no reward of your Father which is in heaven. Matthew 6:1

EMBRACE THE FACT THAT YOU work for the Lord! He is the best employer and overseer! The Lord is your Rewarder and He daily loads you with benefits. Yes, you are subject to lead teachers, administrators, and superintendents but God is The Big Boss. He is called "The Most High" because there is none greater or higher. Although a paycheck may come from your school district, recognize that God is your ultimate source and reward. It is God who approves, validates, and rewards you in ways that extend beyond monetary compensation. Approach your role as an educator with a commitment to excellence recognizing that the quality of your work reflects your devotion to God. Your contributions at your school, no matter how small, are part of a greater purpose aligned to God's plans. Keep the passion for learning and excitement alive in your classroom. Keep your classroom looking fresh and orderly. Let everything you do reflect the integrity and seriousness of your dedication to the Lord. Do not grow weary in well-doing waiting on a thank you or a stamp of approval from others. Spending time with God each day and talking to Him about every detail of your day will help you experience His peace and joy. Set out to be a blessing to students, coworkers, and administrators. Approach each day with the mindset that you are a blessing to those around you. If you never get a thank you from a student, parent, or principal, it is the Lord your God who rewards you. Stay steadfast, unmovable, and always abounding in the work of the Lord, knowing that your efforts in His service are not in vain (1 Corinthians 15:57).

Abba,

I praise Your great and holy name. Thank You for new grace and new mercy for a new day. Thank You for daily loading me with benefits. Thank You for being my Rewarder. You are my portion and the lifter of my head. Before You formed me in my mother's womb You knew me and appointed me for good works. Let me not get discouraged when others do not call my name, approve of me, or give me accolades for my efforts because I know my reward comes from You. I will keep giving and serving my students, their parents, and this community knowing that You are rewarding me in ways that cannot compare to worldly riches.

In Jesus' Name
Amen

Day 18 Celebrate Others

Let nothing be done through strife or vain glory, but in lowliness of mind let each esteem other better than themselves. Philippians 2:3

GOD HAS GIVEN YOU THE grace and mercy needed to fulfill your calling as an educator. Do not try to emulate others or compare yourself to others. In education, there is space for collaboration, not for comparison and competition. Educators can destroy school morale by being proud, competitive, and jealous of each other. Show up each day as God's unique creation, knowing you are the only one who can run the race set before you. If you are sharing a lesson plan as a grade level or instructional strategy, remember that only you can teach it like you. New teachers should not compare themselves to veteran educators. The Bible is clear that believers should humble themselves and think of others as better than themselves. Any form of competition should only be for fun and laughter. When you go into the classroom each day and close the door, you are working for God and not as a show for others. On a teaching team or a grade level, there will be teachers with various strengths and gifts. One teacher may have a strength in management, another in technology, and another in teaching methods. Through collaboration and teamwork, these diverse strengths can come together to create an educational experience that profoundly impacts the lives of students, benefiting the entire team, grade level, and school. Spending time with God in the secret place will help you to see your gifts and recognize the gifts and strengths in others without competition. Take heed to the warning found in Galatians 5:15, "If you bite and devour one another, take heed that you are not consumed by one another." Make it a habit of celebrating your colleagues creating a culture of peace and collaboration in your school.

Abba,

Thank You for this day. Thank You that You are the God who changes not. Thank You for each student You have chosen for me to teach. Thank You for my school and my coworkers. Thank You that You have not made any mistakes concerning me. I am uniquely designed by You and You are well pleased with me. I cast off the spirits of competition and comparison. Help me to be a blessing to the people in my grade and in my school. I set my eyes on You and I focus on my assignment. I work cooperatively with my coworkers and not in a spirit of competition. I esteem them as better teachers than me. When I go into my classroom, I remember that You are my God and my portion forever.

In Jesus' Name
Amen

Day 19 Fix Your Focus

You will keep him in perfect peace, Whose mind is stayed on You, because he trusts in You. Isaiah 26:3

KEEP YOUR MIND FOCUSED ON the things you can control. Focusing on things beyond your control is a waste of valuable time. Do not focus on what the parent could have done or the decision that the administrator made. Do not focus on the teacher next door, or district leaders and their flaws. There is no perfect school or district. It is so easy to judge but focusing on what other people are doing or not doing will only lead to frustration. The Bible says that God will keep you in perfect peace when your mind stays on Him. Do not get caught in the trap of speaking negatively with colleagues about perceived problems happening in the school or district. Channel this energy in exploring ways to continually improve as a teacher and learn new strategies and skills. Stay abreast of educational trends, connect with online communities, and invest time in reflecting on your journey as an educator. Deliberately share positive aspects and speak well of students and the school. A powerful example was seen in a neighboring school district where teachers initiated a "Positive Vibes Challenge" to combat low morale. Starting with small steps, such as sharing positive moments at the beginning of each meeting, this initiative gradually transformed into "Staff Spotlights" celebrating successes and fostering a culture of appreciation. The initiative started small but eventually transformed the school's culture. Teachers found renewed energy and enthusiasm in their work. Consider starting a personal challenge by dedicating yourself to focusing on and sharing the good. Keep your mind filled with thoughts of peace and love. By choosing to focus on the positive aspects of your school, you contribute to a culture of optimism and growth.

Abba,

You have said that if I keep my mind on You, You will keep me in perfect peace. I set my focus and attention on You. You are worthy of my praise and my adoration. Thank You for providing peace that passes all understanding. Father, I trust You and trust that You are taking care of me. I keep my mind on things above where Christ is (Col. 3:1-3). I will not focus my mind on school leaders and what they are doing or not doing. I pray that You will be a hedge of protection over my school. I pray for the leaders in my school and district, and I pray that You will give them the wisdom and guidance to make decisions. I choose to focus my mind on the things that I can control in my classroom. I thank You that You are causing all things to work together for good.

In Jesus' Name
Amen

Day 20 – You are Human

Seeing that we have a great High Priest, that is passed into the heavens, Jesus the Son of God, let us hold fast to our confession. Let us therefore come boldly unto the throne of grace, that we may obtain mercy, and find grace to help in our time of need.
Hebrews 4:14 & 16 (NKJV)

ACCEPT THE FACT THAT THERE will be days that you will mess up! You are human; not perfect, and you will make mistakes in your personal and professional lives. The key is to focus on learning from these mistakes rather than dwelling on them. Just as you encourage your students, openly acknowledge your errors, and find humor in your mistakes. In such an atmosphere students feel comfortable taking risks and admitting errors. This fosters an environment of continuous learning – through trial and error. Grant yourself forgiveness when needed, whether it is for reacting in anger, missing a deadline, or making other errors. If your actions have caused harm, take ownership, seek forgiveness from both the person involved and from God, and then move forward. Recognize that perfection is unattainable, and mistakes provide valuable opportunities for improvement. Model a positive response to errors, demonstrating to students that learning is an ongoing process for everyone, including teachers. It is human nature to avoid the time of solitude and reflection with The Creator after missing the mark. Resist this urge and instead, follow the encouragement from today's scripture to go quickly and boldly to God's throne for help in your time of need. Do not make the mistake of missing one day of sitting at His feet due to a mistake. Take confidence in the words, "If we confess our sins, He is faithful and just to forgive us our sins, and to cleanse us from all unrighteousness" (1 John 1:9). Accept God's grace and mercy that is available to you because of the finished work of Jesus. Remember that your role as an educator includes modeling Godly character and a mindset of lifelong learning.

Abba,

Thank You for the finished work of Jesus on the cross. I come boldly to Your throne to ask You to forgive me for a rebellious heart. Thank You for the voice of the Holy Spirit that convicts me of my sins. I confess these sins to You, and I accept Your grace and mercy. Your Word says if we confess our sins, You are faithful to forgive. I forgive myself and understand that You do not expect perfection from me. Thank You for Your faithfulness to me. Help me to always stand ready to forgive others the way you forgive me.

In Jesus' Name
Amen.

Day 21 Watch Your Thoughts

Finally, brethren, whatsoever things are true, whatsoever things are honest, whatsoever things are just, whatsoever things are pure, whatsoever things are lovely, whatsoever things are of good report; if there be any virtue, and if there be any praise, think on these things. Philippians 4:8

DO YOU OFTEN FIND YOURSELF thinking negatively and critically? Do you constantly think and talk about what students did wrong, the failed lesson, or how the meeting could have been an email? Your thoughts will significantly impact your words and behavior. You will not live a happy and fulfilling life as an educator if you are struggling with negative thoughts and constantly rehearsing what went wrong. In today's scripture, Paul admonishes believers to take control of their thoughts. The Word encourages you to actively think about good things, things that are honest, just, pure, lovely, of good report, virtuous, and praiseworthy. The importance of taking every thought captive (2 Corinthians 10:5), implies that you have the power to proactively manage your thoughts before they take root in your heart. You can intentionally guard yourself from becoming a negative teacher by capturing negative thoughts and deliberately focusing on the positive aspects of your teaching experience. You have the power to choose what you dwell on. You are to dwell on, consider, and meditate on those things that are good and praiseworthy. Think about the student who made you smile, or the parent who expressed words of gratitude for the difference you are making for their child. Consider adopting practices that reinforce positivity, such as keeping a collection of student letters and handwritten notes as sources of inspiration. Engaging in self-care activities is equally important to a positive mindset. Remember to make time for laughter and enjoyment on your journey as an educator, recognizing that your thoughts impact not only your well-being but also the learning environment you create for your students.

Abba,

Thank You for this day. I cast my cares upon You because You care for me. I choose to focus my mind on all the good in my life. Help me to be more aware of my thoughts and to cast down every thought that is not pleasing to You. I want to think about the things that are going well in my classroom, at my school, and in my personal life. As I think about the good, help me to intentionally share the good with others. I thank You for Your goodness and Your mercy. Thank You that nothing can separate me from Your love that is in Christ Jesus.

In Jesus' Name
Amen

Day 22 Enthusiasm

..I am come that they might have life, and that they might have it more abundantly. John 10:10

EFFECTIVE TEACHING NOT ONLY REQUIRES content knowledge, and relationship-building skills but also a generous dose of enthusiasm. Your passion for the subject matter you teach can make learning exciting and fun. When students enjoy the journey of acquiring knowledge, they are more likely to retain information and develop a lifelong love for learning. Having fun with students, whether in the classroom or during recess, is important for building positive relationships and creating an engaging learning environment. When I think of all the educators, I have had the pleasure of knowing, I have fond memories of the ones with passion and excitement for the profession. Their passion was contagious and helped to contribute to a positive school culture. In reflecting upon the importance of enthusiasm in education, I am reminded of the education guru Ron Clark, who is an advocate of having enthusiasm in the learning process. His story demonstrates the positive impact of adding music, dance, and passion to motivate and inspire students. Visiting the Ron Clark Academy and witnessing the contagious energy and genuine joy infused into the educational process left an enduring impact on me. In his book, *"The Excellent 11: An Award-Winning Teacher's Guide to Motivate, Inspire, and Educate Kids,"* Clark emphasizes the importance of teachers creating a classroom that is comfortable, inspired, and enthusiastic, given the significant time spent there. He encourages active participation in dress-up days, pep rallies, and other enjoyable school activities. In line with this, remembering that Jesus came so that we might enjoy life abundantly, encourages you to make every day in the classroom an opportunity to share that joy and excitement with your students. The memories created in a positive and enjoyable classroom environment have the potential to last a lifetime.

Abba

You reign over all the Earth. Thank You for this day. Thank You that Jesus came so that I might enjoy an abundant life. Show me how to relax and enjoy my students and this season of my life. Thank You for Your unconditional love. I put my complete trust in You as my source. Help me to love Your people and have compassion for them like Jesus did. Thank You that Jesus is my model and standard. Help me to walk worthy and pleasing before You. Give me the wisdom to deal with every situation and to create a classroom that is fun, fair, and consistent.

In Jesus' Name
Amen

Day 23 Locos Parentis

.. Thou shalt love thy neighbor as thyself. Matthew 22:39

I LOVE HEARING TEACHERS REFER to their students as "my babies" or "my kids." I also find it funny when a child accidentally calls a teacher Mom or Dad. The Latin phrase locos parentis means "in the place of a parent." The phrase refers to one's legal responsibility to take on the role of the parent when children are under their care. The law states that when parents send their children to school, they are extending their authority to educators and administrators. It is the expectation that educators would treat children as if they were their own children. Similarly, The Word teaches that you should love your neighbor as you love yourself. Experiencing a deep sense of maternal or paternal instincts toward students is natural and fosters a strong commitment to their well-being and academic growth. If you feel anger or animosity towards a child or the children you teach, release those emotions to God. It will be hard to exercise the concept of locos parentis with children if you harbor negative emotions for them. It's okay to confess these feelings to God, He already knows. Students may not remember the specific things that you taught them, but they will always remember how you treated them. Teachers sometimes feel bad to admit that there are some days they would rather stay home, and there are some students who are hard to like or even love. Those are the very children who need the most love. Extend to these children the love that God sent sending His Son to die for sinners. God expects you to love like He loved. God so loved the world, that He gave His only Son (John 3:16). Remember, as a teacher, you have the power to influence a child's life in ways that will last a lifetime. Treat them with love and care, just like they were your own.

Abba,

I praise You and thank You that in this changing world, You change not. You are the same yesterday, today, and forever. You have commanded me to love my neighbor as myself. To treat others with the same care and love that I treat myself. Help me to love my students as if they were my personal children. Show me how to communicate this love to my students both verbally and non-verbally. Even when they disobey or rebel against my authority, help me to always have a plan of redemption for them the same way You had a plan of redemption for humanity through Your Son, Jesus. I surrender my emotions to You, and I confess that there are students that I sometimes don't like. Help me to remember that You loved me when I was not loveable. Give me a heart of flesh that looks at my students with the same level of compassion as Jesus.

In Jesus' Name
Amen

Day 24 Anxious for Nothing

Be anxious for nothing, but in everything, by prayer and supplication with thanksgiving, let your requests be made known to God. and the peace of God, which surpasses all understanding, will guard your hearts and minds through Christ Jesus. Philippians 4:6-7.

THE DEMANDS OF TEACHING CAN feel overwhelming, leading to anxiety and stress. Fortunately, the guidance provided in today's scripture offers a powerful solution. The reminder to "be anxious for nothing" encourages educators to lean on the promises of God. Jesus invites us to cast our cares upon Him, assuring us that He will carry our burdens. You can feel a sense of relief when you recognize that the responsibility of educating God's children does not rest solely on your shoulders. The battle belongs to the Lord, and God extends an offer to carry the burdens of the job. Embrace this offer by entrusting every aspect of your teaching journey to Him. To alleviate the constant presence of job-related concerns in your mind, practice giving those worries to God. Allow Him to work through you in the daily tasks of planning lessons, conducting activities, and fostering a positive learning environment. Develop effective planning strategies to minimize last-minute stress. Create a weekly or monthly schedule, allowing time for preparation, grading, and personal activities. Ask God for creative and effective ways to engage your students in learning. God wants you to pray about every detail and every situation. You can pray over every lesson plan, every faculty meeting, and every parent conference. God has offered "rest" and "relief" in Him. At the end of each day, talk to God acknowledge your challenges and needs, then consciously decide to let go of the worries of the day. Cast all your anxiety on Him because He cares for you.

Abba,

I praise You that You are the Living God who neither slumbers nor sleeps. I thank You for Jesus' sacrifice which gives me access to come to You in prayer about the things that I am anxious about. I thank You that You have commanded us to be anxious for nothing but to come to You in prayer with thanksgiving and to let my request be made known to You. I confess that I am anxious about this assignment and concerned about the children that You have assigned to me. Thank You for reminding me that the children and their parents all belong to You and You are working all things for my good. I cast my cares on to You because You care about me. Show me how to give You every child, every situation, and every detail of the job. Thank You that You have promised to carry these things for me and that I don't have to allow them to stress me out. I cast these cares upon You, and I receive Your victory and Your rest.

In Jesus' Name
Amen

Day 25 Teachable Moments

Give instruction to a wise man, and he will be still wiser; teach a just man, and he will increase in learning. Proverbs 9:9

A "TEACHABLE MOMENT" IS A situation that arises in the classroom, which allows an opportunity to teach biblical principles. You will have many opportunities to teach your students biblical life lessons using everyday language without quoting scriptures. By pausing to capture these moments, you will reinforce the importance of values and model God's nature to children. Whether it is during routine activities such as lining up, sharing assignments, taking turns, or collaborating on tasks, these moments offer a tangible way to model biblical principles. During my highly anticipated frog dissection lesson, I noticed one student, Michael, nervously fidgeting with the dissection tray, communicating his unease at the idea of dissecting the frog. Recognizing that there may be other students facing the same fears, I paused the lesson and took the time to share the story of when I was faced with dissecting my first frog and how I eventually found confidence and fascination in the process. Capturing this teachable moment imparted a valuable lesson to Michael about courage, perseverance, and the beauty of scientific inquiry, but it also reminded me of how far I had come and the transformative power of facing challenges with determination and an open mind. Seek guidance from God on how to leverage these opportunities in everyday classroom interactions. When possible, be strategic about incorporating literature or stories that convey moral lessons that align with biblical principles. Discussing the characters' choices and consequences allows students to explore ethical considerations in a narrative context. These teachable moments can be incorporated into any school routine, no matter how busy. By weaving biblical principles into your teaching in these practical ways, you can create a classroom environment that not only educates academically but also nurtures the moral and ethical character of your students.

Abba,

Thank You that this profession gives me the ability to influence Your younger children. Help me to take advantage of teachable moments in my classroom to model Your principles for Godly living. Give me eyes to see and ears to hear as I model Your love in my classroom. Season my words so that others may taste and see that You are good. I ask that You help me to always remain teachable and not be wise in my own eyes. Help me to always remember that just like the children are learning from me; I am also learning from them and others. You are The Master Teacher; help me to be a model of Your love and grace in my classroom.

In Jesus' Name,
Amen

Day 26 Choose Love

And though I have the gift of prophecy, and understand all mysteries and all knowledge; and though I have all faith, so that I could remove mountains, but have not charity, I am nothing. 1 Corinthians 13:2

GOD IS LOVE, AND AS a teacher, your calling is twofold: to serve and, most importantly, to love. You can have the best lesson plans, the best instructional strategies, and the best-looking classroom, but if there is no love you will be ineffective! While subject matter expertise is important, teaching involves more than just conveying information. It is a commitment to understanding, supporting, and inspiring every student on their unique educational path. A teacher's love for students creates a connection that goes beyond the curriculum. Let love serve as your guiding principle, shaping decision-making and interactions. It should also influence the tone of the classroom, your approach to discipline, and how challenges are addressed. If love is in your heart, it will flow through your verbal and non-verbal communication with students, their parents, and stakeholders. Jesus said that people would know that we are His disciples by how we love one another (John 13:35). God, in sending His

Son Jesus to the cross for sinners, set the standard for love. Love enables teachers to see the potential in every student, fostering a belief that everyone can succeed and make a positive contribution to society. In essence, love stands as the heartbeat of effective teaching, elevating your classroom to a place where students not only gain knowledge but also experience care, encouragement, and a profound sense of belonging. When students feel loved, they will engage freely in the learning process, and you will leave a positively powerful impact.

Abba,

Thank You that You are love. Thank You that You so loved the world that You gave us the gift of Your Son. Father, Your Word is clear if I don't have love, I am nothing. Give me a heart of love for Your children and the education profession. Thank You that on the difficult days, You have promised that You will never leave me or forsake me. You are on my side and causing all things to work together for my good. I choose to love Your people. I choose to push past my emotions and respond in love. I put on Your whole armor so that I can stand each day against the wiles of the enemy. Father today, help me to choose to love no matter the situation. Equip me to respond like Jesus who showed love on His most difficult day.

In Jesus' Name
Amen

Day 27 Positive Mindset

Those things which ye have both learned and received, and heard, and seen in me, do: and the God of peace shall be with you. Philippians 4:9

WHEN LEADERS GIVE YOU ADDITIONAL tasks before you have had the chance to master the things already on your to-do list, it can be overwhelming. What steps should you take when there seems to be insufficient time in the day to meet the current requirements, yet new requirements are being added? Such scenarios are not uncommon in education and can lead to frustration among teachers, to the extent that they hesitate to embrace new initiatives, even if they are beneficial. God has given the solution to every problem in His Word. You should intentionally approach situations like this with a positive mindset. Understand that change is a constant in education, and new initiatives, though challenging, may bring positive outcomes in the long run. Focus on the potential benefits and opportunities for growth. Seeking support and patience during the implementation of new strategies is key. Rather than responding with grumbling or disputing, consider engaging in a respectful and private conversation with school leaders, expressing concerns while emphasizing your commitment to contributing positively. You can rest assured that this new thing will pass away, and something newer will take its place. Follow the biblical guidance to fix your thoughts on things that are good, pure, lovely, and praiseworthy (Philippians 4:8). By adopting a positive mindset, seeking support, and approaching challenges with a solution-oriented mindset, educators can navigate the complexities of the profession while contributing positively to their personal and professional growth.

Abba,

Thank You for this day. Thank You for Your promises to never leave me or forsake me. You know the frustrations and challenges I face in this profession. I cast my cares upon You because You care for me. Give me the right response to additional programs, meetings, or professional development requirements. Help me to always respond appropriately to the people You have placed in authority over me. I cast down every thought that is not pleasing to You and I think about the things that are going well in my classroom, at our school, and in my personal life. I choose to think about the good and intentionally share the good. I thank You for Your goodness and Your mercy. Thank You that nothing can separate me from Your love that is in Christ Jesus.

In Jesus' Name
Amen

Day 28 Power of Prayer

And He spake a parable unto them to this end that men ought always to pray, and not to faint. Luke 18:1

THE LYRICS OF THE SONG *"What a Friend We Have in Jesus"* incorporate the line, "Oh, what needless pain we bear, all because we fail to bring everything to God in prayer." The song suggests that unnecessary pain is often endured because we fail to bring everything to God in prayer, leading to a loss of inner peace. In line with today's scripture, Jesus admonished the disciples to always pray and never give up. Jesus knew how vital and important a life of prayer is for believers. Many educators go home thinking about their students and are always looking for ways to improve. The fact that the job is on your mind after hours is an indication that you need to pray. Prayer allows you to unload your burdens on God. When thoughts about your school day come to mind after hours make this your cue to pray. You cannot afford to neglect your quiet time of prayer. One challenging semester a close teacher friend, Sarah, found herself facing an unexpected personal crisis. She was dealing with health issues that made it increasingly difficult for her to maintain a work-life balance. Feeling overwhelmed by the responsibilities of teaching and the demands of her personal life, Sarah sought refuge in prayer, pouring out her heart to God. Every morning before heading to school, she found a quiet moment to pray and draw from the Well of Living Water. In the days that followed, Sarah noticed that her prayers had changed from prayers of desperation to prayers of gratitude. She realized that God had answered her cries for help. The challenges had not vanished, but they appeared more as stepping stones rather than stumbling blocks. Like Sarah you may feel an overwhelming burden in your personal or professional life. Allow God to carry the burden of educating His children by taking all your issues to Him in prayer. Follow Jesus' command in today's scripture, to always pray and not give up.

Abba,

You are my peace, and You are my strength for the journey. I come to You to pray about all the details of my job as a teacher. I thank You that there is no problem too large or too small that You won't hear. I thank You that You have commanded me to be anxious for nothing but to come to You in prayer with thanksgiving and to let my requests be made known to You. Show me how to consistently give You every child, every situation, and every detail of the job. I thank You that the battle belongs to You. Thank You that You have promised to carry even my battles. I thank You that You are all-seeing and all-knowing God. Thank You for the victory and for Your rest.

In Jesus' Name
Amen

Day 29 Power, Love, & A Sound Mind

For God has not given us a spirit of fear; but of power, and love, and of a sound mind. 2 Timothy 1:7

BY NOW YOU HAVE LIKELY forgotten the inspirational messages from the beginning of the semester. More than inspirational messages or dynamic professional development, educators need ongoing power that comes only from God. You must embrace and connect to the divine strength that lies within you. Recognize that the power within you surpasses your human abilities. The same power that raised Jesus from the dead lives on the inside of you (Romans 8:11). In moments of fear, weakness, or feeling inadequate, it is crucial to remember that God has given you a spirit of power, love, and a sound mind. The promise is particularly reassuring when the days as a teacher include meeting deadlines, multitasking, and emotional resilience. Trust in the understanding that you are not alone, God is with you in your classroom strengthening you and guiding you throughout the day. Whisper prayers of gratitude throughout the day thanking God. Surround yourself with scriptures or affirmations that align with your faith and values. Place them in visible locations, such as on your desk or computer, to serve as constant reminders of your faith in God. Foster connections with Christian colleagues. Engage in discussions, share experiences, and support one another spiritually. Remember you must take intentional moments of stillness daily to connect with this wellspring of power. Ask God for a renewal and a rekindling of the passion that led you to the teaching profession in the first place. Embrace the divine strength within you, allowing it to guide you through each day with confidence, love, and a sound mind.

Abba,

I praise You that You are God alone. There is nothing too hard for You. You have no rivals, and You have no equals. There is none like You in all the Earth. I thank You for this day. I thank You that I am fearfully and wonderfully made. I thank You that You have blotted out all of my transgressions. Today, I come to exchange my fears and insecurities for Your power and love. I submit myself to Your will for my life. Thank You that the same power that raised Jesus from the dead lives on the inside of me. I choose to think of the promises of Your Word. I ask you to renew my passion for this profession each day. Thank You that You have equipped me to do Your will and to teach Your children. Today, I choose to follow Your will and Your plans for my life.

In Jesus' Name
Amen

Day 30 Opening Doors of Opportunity

...You have not, because you ask not. – James 4:2

WHAT SPECIFIC NEEDS DO YOU have today? Perhaps you need resources for a project, tips for reaching a challenging student, or a breakthrough in your teaching methods. Have you taken the time to bring these concerns to God? Remember, The Creator of the universe resides within you through the indwelling Holy Spirit—a boundless source of answers to every question. Ask Him for the wisdom to plan and implement your lessons in a manner that students can understand. Ask Him to show you how to acquire the resources that you need for His children. Today's scripture emphasizes the fact that often believers have not simply because they are not making the request. I recall my days working with a beloved music teacher, Ms. Andrea Nichols who knew the incredible impact of music on her students. Although funds were limited, Ms. Nichols envisioned a music program that would not only foster creativity but also provide a positive outlet for children. After prayer and research, Ms. Nichols took matters into her own hands and began researching grant opportunities. She spent many nights crafting proposals conveying the potential impact of a music program for her students. She received a positive response from a local foundation dedicated to supporting educators. Before long, the joyous sounds of students experimenting with instruments filled the school atmosphere creating a positive learning environment for students (and adults). The music program became a source of pride for the entire school community. Ms. Nichols went on to empower other teachers to write grants to fund their classroom projects. The lesson learned is that sometimes, all it takes is the courage to ask, and doors of opportunity swing open. For everyone who asks receives; he who seeks finds; and to him who knocks, the door will be opened (Matthew 7:8 NKJV).

Abba,

You are the great I AM. I confess that I need Your divine help and wisdom to be the teacher that You have called me to be. I cast my cares and the heavy burden of educating Your children on You. I welcome You into my classroom and accept Your divine assistance. I pray about everything that involves my call to teach Your children. I thank You that there is nothing too small that I can't talk to You about. Thank You for living on the inside of me in the form of the Holy Spirit. Help me to hear Your still small voice with guidance and direction for every detail of my calling. You know my needs and desires; I thank You in advance for the answers to effectively teach Your children. I give You all the glory for the success in my classroom this school year.

In Jesus' Name
Amen

Day 31 A Good Name

A good name is rather to be chosen than great riches, and loving favor rather than silver and gold. Proverbs 22:1

THE SCRIPTURE REMINDS US THAT the worth of a good name far surpasses material wealth. Having a "good name" speaks to your character, reputation, morals, and values. A good name is an important possession for an educator. A reputation for being a good, trustworthy, and fair teacher is imperative. Throughout my years as an administrator, the beginning of each school year was always marked by a flood of parental requests for specific teachers. These requests underscore the impact of a teacher's reputation on shaping the choices and expectations of families seeking the best for their children. The influence of a teacher's reputation extends far beyond parental requests; it also has a profound impact on enrollment numbers and the trust parents place in the school and district's ability to provide a quality education. Maintaining a positive reputation involves more than adhering to professional codes and attending mandatory ethics training. It is an ongoing commitment to embodying the values of competence, integrity, and fairness in every aspect of life. Strive for excellence each day in your classroom, be a person of your word, and treat others with respect, regardless of their position. Remember that a positive reputation not only speaks volumes about an educator's ability to teach but also influences the overall perception of the education profession. As ambassadors of Christ, we represent Him not only within the confines of our classrooms but in every area of our lives. By living according to God's Word, we will not only adhere to ethical standards but live a life that represents Christ well, attracting others to the life-changing power of following Him.

Abba,

Thank You for this day. Help me to live a life that is worthy of the high calling of Christ. Help me to listen to the voice of the Holy Spirit and to avoid all appearances of evil. Just like Jesus lowered Himself and became a man, I lower myself as Your servant today. I esteem others as higher and better than myself. I set out to be the best teacher I can be for You and not for recognition from people. I thank You that You are my Rewarder, and I am Your representative in my classroom and in this school today. I thank You all things are working for good.

In Jesus' Name
Amen

Day 32 Self-Care

And He said unto them, "Come aside by yourselves to a deserted place and rest a while," For there were many coming and going, and they did not have time to eat." Mark 6:31

TEACHING IS A REWARDING YET demanding profession that can often exceed the standard 40-hour work week. Many dedicated educators find themselves working tirelessly juggling responsibilities—teaching, family, church, afterschool activities, and personal pursuits—often neglecting the crucial need for relaxation. This persistent pace can lead to stress, frustration, and ultimately burnout. Some teachers may find themselves like hamsters on a wheel of constant activity, not realizing the necessity of resting to be more productive. In today's scripture, Jesus admonished His disciples to take a break and rest. Jesus gave these men work to do, but He also called them to step aside and rest for a while. You have been called to the ministry work of teaching, like the disciples, Jesus also wants you to take time to recharge your battery and refresh your soul. Make it a priority to leave work at a set time each day and to carve out time on the weekends for rest and to do things that you enjoy. Grant yourself the grace to take personal leave days without guilt. Release the worry about what happens at the school when you are not present—everything will be there waiting upon your return. In the book, *"180 Days of Self-Care for Busy Educators,"* Tina Boogren emphasizes the importance of educators prioritizing self-care to present their best selves to those they serve and love. Boogren offers practical, low-cost strategies for supporting educators' health and well-being. She further encourages educators to break free from device addiction and the constant need to be doing something. It is essential to recognize the importance of rest, even God took time to rest after completing His work (Genesis 2:2). Align yourself to the rhythm of God, avoiding the tendency to overextend to the point of stress and lack of productivity. Spending time in communion with your Creator is the ultimate form of self-care.

Abba,

Thank You for this day. Thank You for new grace and new mercy. Thank You for loading me with benefits daily. You are my portion and the lifter of my head. Before You formed me in my mother's womb You knew me and appointed me for good works. Show me how to balance my time to be productive for Your Kingdom. Show me how to learn to rest in You and not stress over the things I cannot control. Help me to not seek reward from man, I choose to put my focus and attention on things above. I trust what you are doing in this season of my life.

In Jesus' Name
Amen

Day 33 Quick to Listen

Everyone should be quick to listen, slow to speak, and slow to anger. James 1:19 (NIV)

THE ABILITY TO LISTEN IS an important trait for a teacher. When you truly listen to someone, you do more than hear their words; you give the person your full attention. You register not just what they are saying, but also what their body language is communicating to you. In today's scripture, James encourages the believers to be quick to hear and slow to speak. Take the time to listen to your students, parents, and school leaders. Listening to students will help you better understand how to pray for them and how to meet unspoken needs. It is also important that you do not do all the talking in your classroom, but you allow space for the students to have an active voice. Creating opportunities for students to talk and listen to each other can also foster a collaborative learning environment and improve communication skills. Disciplining yourself to listen more than you talk is a powerful practice. Do not listen to respond but listen to understand. In staff development and professional learning opportunities, be open-minded and teachable. In my own experience as an administrator, I've learned that the effectiveness of teachers is not necessarily linked to the volume of their voices in meetings. True power lies in disciplined listening and a lot can be learned when a person disciplines themselves to listen more than talking. Michael Linsin in *"Happy Teacher Habits,"* suggests that cultivating good listening skills can enhance your effectiveness as a colleague, elevate your performance, and contribute to overall job satisfaction. Wise people have learned that more wisdom can be gained by listening, observing, and not rushing to speak. Even in Your quiet time with God, take time to read His Word and listen. When there are many words, transgression is unavoidable, but he who restrains his lips is wise (Proverbs 10:19 NKJV).

Abba,

I praise You, The All Sufficient One. You are my ever-present help in times of trouble. I come to abide myself in You and I remember that apart from You, I can do nothing. You know the plans and the purpose that You have for me. In all situations, help me to be slow to speak, quick to listen, and slow to become angry. Thank You that I don't have to always give my opinion or thoughts on a matter. I need Your help to show me how to create lessons that will allow students to talk and share. Thank You for equipping me to teach Your students. May Your will be done today.

In Jesus' Name
Amen

Day 34 Working with Excellence

Whatever You do, work at it with all your heart, as working for the Lord, not for human masters, since You know that you will receive an inheritance from the Lord as a reward. It is the Lord Christ you are serving. Colossians 3:23-24 (NIV)

THE BIBLE IS CLEAR THAT we should work with all our hearts unto the Lord and not for man. Our ultimate purpose is to please God and not man. When you are teaching your students, you are working for God and not for your school principal or superintendent. Do not look for accolades from man but work as unto the Lord. Your Heavenly Father who sees what you do secretly will reward you openly. You should not teach with a different level of passion and enthusiasm when there are observers in your classroom. As educators, it is essential to avoid putting on a show, aligning with the biblical principle found in Matthew 6:1-4. In this scripture, Jesus warns against practicing righteousness to be seen by others, emphasizing that if a person does good deeds for public recognition, they have already received their reward. Your actions, including teaching, should be motivated by a sincere desire to serve and please God rather than seeking praise or recognition from others. Your best lessons will take place when there is no one in the classroom, but you, your students, and of course the Lord. Remember, God is omnipresent, and He will never leave you or forsake you. He is always present, and He sees and knows all. Ask God to help you to always give your best for His Glory. When observers come to your classroom as required for observation and coaching, it should be a business-as-usual atmosphere because God is your real boss, and He is the one who sustains you and rewards you. The promise of receiving an inheritance from the Lord as a reward is a testament that your efforts are recognized and will be rewarded.

Abba,

Thank You for my job, this school, and this school district. Help me to always honor You in my work. Help me to not work for the approval of man but work to honor You. Help me to always remember that You are present with me in my classroom each day. You see everything I do and You hear everything that is said. Help me to not be satisfied with giving less than my best. Help me to plan lessons and activities that will honor You. Help me to be a person of excellence, integrity, and passion in my classroom as I seek to please You and not man. Thank You for reminding me that my reward comes from You. Help me to always live my life to bring glory to Your name.

In Jesus' Name,
Amen

Day 35 Do Your Homework

Study to shew thyself approved unto God, a workman that needeth not to be ashamed, rightly dividing the word of truth. 2 Timothy 2:15

CONTINUOUS LEARNING AND SELF-IMPROVEMENT ARE critically important, especially for teachers. As an educator, your homework extends beyond studying the Word of God but also includes those seemingly ordinary, yet crucial tasks conducted behind the scenes to ensure a smoothly run classroom. Attending to the little things is a crucial aspect of effective teaching. Doing the homework also means taking the time to properly plan and prepare for each lesson. When you have upcoming trips, events, or parties, take the time to meticulously plan; it is often the little things that become the most important and make the biggest difference. As summer vacation ended each year, lead teacher, Mrs. Charlie Mae Hill would rally her sixth-grade teaching team which included me and several other new teachers to sacrifice a portion of our summer vacation to get a head start on the upcoming school year. Instead of taking a full break, we spent a portion of each summer planning and organizing our classrooms for the new school year. This proactive planning not only saved valuable time during the hectic start of the semester but also translated into a smoother school year. Sacrificing this extra time allowed for a more peaceful start to the school year, freeing me to spend intentional time with God at the beginning of each day. Taking an intentional approach to both my professional and spiritual life created a balance that positively impacted my teaching and the lives of my students. The sacrifice of downtime over the summer for preparation became a rewarding investment and a practice that I embraced throughout my career. Homework for teachers, therefore, means cultivating habits that contribute to a positive and organized learning environment. It is in these seemingly mundane tasks that the foundation for a successful and impactful teaching journey is laid.

Abba,

Thank You for this day. Thank You for Your command to study Your Word and seek You first. Thank You for helping me to be the best teacher that I can be for You. Bring all the little things that need to be done back to my remembrance so that I can create a safe space for Your children. Guide me to use my time wisely so that I am available for the other details of my life. I trust that You are causing all things to work together for my good. I pray for my students, parents, and colleagues at this school. May Your will be done in every classroom.

In Jesus' Name
Amen

Day 36 Unity in the School Family

Behold, how good and how pleasant it is For brethren to dwell together in unity. Psalm 133:1

THIS REFLECTIVE STATEMENT BEAUTIFULLY CAPTURES the essence of the shared journey of educators. In every school, you can witness symbols of unity—mascots, school colors, mottos, and mission statements—all strategically designed to foster a collective sense of purpose and camaraderie. Similarly, within your classroom, grade level, and department, you have the power to cultivate this same spirit and create an educational family. Under the leadership of the late, Mr. Clyde McGrady, Staley Middle School was recognized as a *National School of Excellence* due in part to the overwhelming sense of family that was created leading to high performing culture. By incorporating simple ideas, you can help contribute to an environment of collaboration and support causing the entire team to thrive. Recognize and value the distinctive strengths and skills that each team member brings to the table. Celebrating birthdays and offering support during life's challenges will further nurture the spirit of unity. Even seemingly small acts, such as providing encouragement or covering classes for a bathroom break, can yield a profound influence on

70

the overall culture. Intentionally work to create a sense of unity everywhere that you go. In moments of conflict, be the person who seeks the path of peace, even if it means compromising your desires. I have had the pleasure of developing lifelong friendships by serving alongside other educators in a spirit of unity. As far as it depends on you, strive to live in peace with everyone. (Romans 12:18 NIV). Recognize and embrace the power of unity as a force for collective success. This sense of unity not only enhances the overall school culture but also has a profound impact on student success and well-being. Your school is not just a place of education, it is a surrogate family.

Abba,

I praise You that the Earth is Yours and the fullness thereof. Thank You that this world is not my home. Thank You that I am a part of the larger body of Christ. Show me how to create a sense of community and unity in my classroom, grade level, and school. Thank You for the people You have placed in my grade level and department and the spirit of collaboration. Help me to think of things that are lovely, of good report, and praiseworthy about my school and my job. Above all help me to always remember that I represent You and The Kingdom. May I be an example of your love everywhere I go.

In Jesus' Name
Amen

Day 37 Dress the Part

Therefore, as God's chosen people, holy and dearly loved, clothe yourselves with compassion, kindness, humility, gentleness, and patience. Colossians 3:12 (NIV)

MANY TEACHERS OVERLOOK THE SIGNIFICANCE of dressing professionally, cherishing the occasional days when casual wear, especially jeans, is allowed. I, too, eagerly anticipated casual dress Fridays during my teaching career. However, it is essential to recognize that as a professional, your outward appearance leaves an enduring impression on students and parents alike. The Word reminds us that man judges based on outward appearance, while God looks upon the heart (1 Samuel 16:7). Taking care of your hair, attire, and overall appearance reflects your commitment to your role. You must present yourself professionally, recognizing that you are not just representing the school but also The Kingdom. Your parents, students, and coworkers will respond more positively to you when you "look the part" by dressing professionally each day. According to Harry and Rosemary Wong, in *"The First Days of School, How to be an Effective Teacher,"* when teachers dress professionally, they gain respect and set a positive example for their students. In addition to physically dressing the part of a teacher, today's scripture encourages us to clothe ourselves in the other more important garments of compassion, kindness, humility, gentleness, and patience. These items refer to your overall attitude and behavior. Your attitude should reflect your identity in Christ. The scriptural guidance urges you to let these virtues shape your interactions, guide your decisions, and influence your teaching approach. In doing so, you not only fulfill the role of a teacher but also embody the principles of Christ, creating a positive and impactful presence in the lives of those you teach.

Abba,

You know all and You see all. Nothing is hidden from Your presence. Thank You that You know the end from the beginning. Help me to remember the importance of dressing professionally but also clothing myself in compassion, kindness, humility, gentleness, and patience. I surrender my life to You, and I thank You for redeeming my life from the hand of the enemy. I am not my own, I have been bought with a price. Help me to be a cheerleader for my school, district, and the profession. Thank You for the friend that I have in Jesus. May Your will be done in my life.

In Jesus' Name
Amen.

Day 38 Be Transformed

And be not conformed to this world but be ye transformed by the renewing of your mind, that you may prove what is that good, and acceptable and perfect will of God. Romans 12:2

THIS VERSE IS URGING BELIEVERS not to blindly follow the trends and norms of the world. Instead, it challenges you to be transformed by changing the way you think. This transformation encourages you to question conventional approaches and seek a deeper understanding of God's perspective in your everyday life. For example, many educators find themselves eagerly anticipating the next holiday or counting down the remaining days of the school year. The joy of time away from the classroom can be refreshing but consider a perspective that aligns with the abundant life that Jesus intends. Every day within the walls of your classrooms is an opportunity—a chance to make a lasting impact on young minds. It is easy to get caught up in the routine and yearn for those breaks, but in doing so, you might unintentionally miss the richness and fulfillment that teaching can bring. In essence, the abundant life that Jesus speaks of is not reserved for a distant break or holiday; however, it is a unique part of your everyday experiences as a teacher. Embrace each day as a gift to make a difference in the lives of those entrusted to your care. To genuinely enjoy this abundant life as a teacher, you must transform the way you think by renewing your mind. This also involves being mindful of what you choose to focus on. Instead of dwelling on problems and frustrations, shift your focus to the things that bring joy and fulfillment in your teaching journey. A vital aspect of this renewal is a daily commitment to reading the Bible, allowing the Word to shape and mold you into the image of Jesus. It is through this intentional practice that you can align your thoughts with His teachings and foster a spiritual transformation.

Abba,

I acknowledge that You are the Most High God. You are Alpha and Omega. You are the Beginning and The End. I present myself to You as a living sacrifice. I surrender my mind and my thoughts to You. I allow Your Words to fill my heart and my thoughts. I know that apart from You I can do nothing, and I am nothing. I allow You to transform my thinking as I take on the mind of Christ. Show me the areas in my life where I have not fully surrendered to You. I know that this world is not my home and I do not conform myself to the ways of this world. Forgive me for the ways that I fail You each day. Lead me in the way everlasting.

In Jesus' Name
Amen

Day 39 Taste & See

O taste and see that the LORD is good; Blessed is the man that trusteth in Him. Psalm 34:8

THIS PSALM IS AN INVITATION to experience God firsthand. Consider it as God's way of saying, "Experience my goodness in your teaching journey." Just like enjoying a delicious meal at your favorite restaurant, savor the goodness in the connections with students, the support of the school community, and the power you have to shape futures. This perspective turns each day into a flavorful experience of God's abundant goodness. The takeaway is a practical commitment to slow down and appreciate the moments of your daily routines, recognizing self-awareness as a crucial aspect of a fulfilling and balanced life. And when things get a little crazy (as they often do), remember to take refuge in the Lord. Find strength, wisdom, and a sense of peace in His presence. Your teaching journey is a daily adventure. Appreciate each student's uniqueness, collaborate with colleagues, and recognize the impact you make every day. Do not forget to jot down reflections, challenges faced, and moments of gratitude in your journal each day. This can serve as a form of prayerful reflection and a way to invite God into your professional experiences. Remember, spending time with God is essential for your well-being and survival. It is not merely an option but a necessity. In His presence, there is fullness of joy, and at His right hand, there are pleasures for evermore (Psalm 16:11). As you navigate the twists and turns of this academic adventure, remember to taste, and see. Take refuge in the Lord amid challenges, finding strength, wisdom, and a sense of peace. Let today's scripture guide you on your teaching journey.

Abba,

I praise You for Your goodness. There is none like You in all the Earth. You are great and greatly to be praised. I have tasted and we have seen that You are good. Thank You for Your goodness to me and humankind. I invite You into the details of my day as a teacher for Your Kingdom. Give me the wisdom I need to meet the needs of Your children. Thank You that You will never leave me or forsake me and that You are with me through each minute of the day. Today I acknowledge that You are my strength and my salvation. You are my refuge and my strong tower. Apart from You, I can do nothing. May the people around me see Your light in me.

In Jesus' Name
Amen

Day 40 Calm Anger

Be ye angry, and sin not: let not the sun go down on your
wrath: neither give place to the devil. Ephesians 4:26-27

ANGER IS A COMMON HUMAN emotion. Even Jesus became angry (Mark 3:5). However, as a teacher and follower of Christ, you must learn to manage your anger, or it will manage you. How will you respond when that student or parent triggers feelings of anger in you? Never forget that you are modeling correct behavior and young people are watching your response. Uncontrolled anger is unbecoming of a follower of Christ. Jesus showed controlled anger in turning over the tables of the tax collectors (John 2:15). Recognizing that anger and hatred are emotionally and physically draining, James 3:16 warns that envy and strife breed confusion and every evil work. Never get into power struggles with children. It is okay for you to allow them to have the last word and walk away and document the incident. Uncontrolled and unresolved anger will lead to sin. It is best to keep quiet when you become angry because you are more likely to say or do something you might regret later. When there is a conflict with students or adults, look for ways to manage the problem without escalating the conflict. In his book *"What Great Teachers Do*

Differently: 17 Things that Matter Most". Todd Whitaker offers a solution for educators when dealing with aggressive parents. According to Whitaker, an educator can listen to the parent's concerns and respond with "I am sorry that happened." Whitaker further states that this is not accepting or placing blame but is a great way to diffuse a difficult situation. Educators practice wisdom when they do not immediately respond with a defensive stance but operate in love. Today's scripture emphasizes not allowing anger to lead to sin and encourages a swift resolution rather than harboring anger all day.

Abba,

I acknowledge that You are the Most High God. You are Alpha and Omega. You are The Beginning and The End. I present myself to You as a living sacrifice. I surrender my mind and my thoughts to You. I allow Your Words to fill my heart and my thoughts. I know that apart from You I can do nothing, and I am nothing. I allow You to transform my thinking as I take on the mind of Christ. Teach me to appropriately handle situations in my life that make me. Forgive me for the ways that I fail You each day. Help me to walk in forgiveness with others. May Your will be done in my life.

In Jesus' Name
Amen

Day 41 Never Defeated

We are troubled on every side, yet not distressed: we are perplexed but not in despair, persecuted, but not forsaken; cast down but not destroyed; always bearing about in the body the dying of the Lord Jesus, that the life of Jesus might be manifest in our body. - 2 Corinthians 4:8-10

DESPITE THE DIFFICULTIES YOU MAY face today, you are not abandoned or destroyed. The strength of Jesus Christ empowers you to overcome all the frustrations and challenges of the profession. Today's verses resonate with the challenges often faced by many educators. In my teaching journey, one of the toughest moments came when I was abruptly moved from the sixth-grade teaching team to the seventh-grade team. Learning a new curriculum and facing the prospect of teaching the same students for a second year initially left me disheartened and frustrated. My love for my previous team and the uncertainty of the future filled me with fear. Having the summer after the announcement to rest and reflect gave me time to shift my focus and see things from God's perspective. In the end, what initially seemed like a difficulty transformed into an opportunity. The students flourished and the new teaching team welcomed me warmly. I emerged stronger and happier realizing that God had a purpose in redirecting my path. Over my 32 years in education, I have had similar experiences that included changing schools and districts. Though painful at the time, looking back, I can see how those seemingly difficult changes paved the way for a richer and more fulfilling career. These experiences taught me the importance of trusting in God's plan and finding strength in unexpected changes. As an educator, you may also encounter unexpected shifts or challenges, and it is in those moments that you may feel that your faith is tested. No matter the challenges you are currently facing, today's scripture serves as a powerful reminder that you are an overcomer in Christ.

Abba,

I praise You that You are the "All Sufficient One". You are my sustainer and provider. I declare today that I can do all things through Christ who strengthens me. Thank You that no matter the challenges of this day, You have promised that You will never leave me or forsake me. You are my refuge and my strength. Thank You that You are on my side and causing all things to work together for my good. Thank You that despite the challenges in school and life, as Your child, I am never defeated.

In Jesus' Name
Amen

Day 42 Liberation in Christ

blotting out the handwriting of ordinances that was against us, which was contrary to us, and took it out of the way, nailing it to the cross. Colossians 2:14

NO MATTER WHAT LEVEL YOU teach, there are rules and expectations for behavior in your classroom or school. Students are expected to follow these standards whether or not they understand or agree with them. Broken rules in school, at home, or even in society result in negative consequences. In the Old Testament, God established rules and laws for humanity. Due to the inherent sinful nature, these rules proved challenging for people to uphold. The Bible affirms that all individuals have fallen short and sinned. Thankfully, the redemptive act of Jesus' sacrifice on the cross served to pardon man's sin debt, providing a path to forgiveness. He was wounded for our transgressions; he was bruised for our iniquities and the chastisement of our peace was upon Him (Isaiah 53:5). So how do you respond when students break the rules? Respond with the same grace and mercy that has been extended to you through Jesus. While you must have consequences, implement these consequences considering the love of God to you. As an administrator, I was faced with an unexpected challenge when

Aniyah, a typically well-behaved student, was sent to the office for breaking a rule. Rather than immediately invoking consequences, I sensed there was more to the story. In a brief conversation, Aniyah disclosed the recent loss of a close family member and the resulting emotional turmoil. While consequences for breaking the rule were still necessary, it was equally vital to approach this situation with a mindset that prioritized support and care. In this moment, Aniyah needed more than disciplinary action; she needed a supportive environment that acknowledged her struggles and provided a path toward healing. By responding to rule violations with compassion and restorative measures, you can create spaces where students can find support, healing, and the opportunity to overcome personal challenges.

Abba,

Thank You that I have a new life in Jesus Christ. I thank You that Jesus became sin for me so that I could be made righteous in You. Help me to extend the same grace and mercy to others that You have extended to me through Jesus. I declare that I am crucified with Christ, but I live but it is not I, but I allow Jesus to live through me. I surrender my eyes, my hands, my feet, and my voice for Your service. I offer myself as an act of worship to You. Thank You for Jesus' model of obedience. I humble myself for Your service. Give me a spirit of obedience to Your voice. May Your will be done in my life.

In Jesus' Name
Amen

Day 43 Have Patience

The Lord is not slack concerning his promise, as some men count slackness; but is longsuffering to us-ward, not willing that any should perish, but that all should come to repentance.
2 Peter 3:9

TEACHING IS A JOURNEY MARKED by promises—promises of growth, learning, and the positive impact you can make on the lives of your students. However, the path to realizing these promises is often filled with challenges, setbacks, and moments that test your patience. Our scripture from Peter offers a valuable perspective as we navigate these times. As you strive to create environments of learning and growth in your classroom, remember the importance of patience. Be patient with yourself as you refine your teaching methods and extend patience to your students as they navigate their distinctive paths of understanding. Just as the Lord is patient with you, you are called to extend that same patience to students and coworkers. How can you foster patience during difficult circumstances? As you wait for that student to finish their statement, instead of checking your watch in frustration, say a quiet prayer to calm your heart. As you wait for the last student to finish the assignment, check in with the student who has been absent for a few days. Teaching is not a sprint but rather a marathon—a journey that requires endurance, patience, and a steadfast commitment to the growth of every student. Embrace the journey, trusting that your patience will play a role in fostering the full potential of your students. Every student can learn but each will learn at a different pace, be patient with the process. Remember that God demonstrates patience with you and orchestrates events in His perfect timing. As today's scripture states God is patient, and does not wish that any should perish, but that all should reach repentance. In moments of challenge and waiting, let this scripture remind you to trust in the Lord's timing and extend the same patience and understanding to those around you.

Abba,

I come to acknowledge that You are the Living God. You are the Ancient of Days. I Thank You for Your Son, Jesus. Thank You for being patient with me. Help me to be patient with my students, coworkers, and family members. Help me to show the same grace and mercy that You have so graciously given to me. Help me to never give up on any of my students like You never give up on me. You have specifically assigned them to me for a purpose. Help me to walk in the Spirit and to display patience with everyone that I come into contact with. May they see You in me.

In Jesus' Name
Amen

Day 44 Create the Good

But do not forget to do good and to share, for with such sacrifices God is well pleased. Hebrews 13:16

THIS VERSE SERVES AS A reminder of the impact your acts of kindness and generosity can have on your classroom and the entire school community. You have the power to create an atmosphere of goodness and sharing that goes beyond the classroom. Whether it is offering extra help, lending a listening ear, or the countless moments that you go above and beyond to support your students. Make sure your classroom is filled with an atmosphere of positive words and an uplifting spirit. Consider starting the day with a brief morning meeting where students share positive experiences and accomplishments or express gratitude. This sets a positive tone for the day. Be intentional about creating lessons that are engaging and allow all students to experience success. Creating lessons that will intentionally produce success for students will build confidence and self-esteem. Displaying student work serves as another great form of encouragement. Implement a positive reinforcement system where positive actions are recognized and celebrated. *In "The Burnout Cure Learning to Love Teaching Again",* author Chase Mielke suggests that teachers must be "goodness curators" orchestrating moments of triumph and memories of affirmation for students. By following these principles, teachers contribute to both academic growth and the overall development of their students. Cultivating a positive classroom environment serves as a force that goes beyond academics. As you continue to do good and share with your students, remember that God is pleased with such acts of kindness.

Abba,

I praise You that You are the same yesterday, today, and forever, I praise You that You are the God who changes not. Thank You that You are the God who leaves the 99 to go after the one. You stand at the door, and You knock. Show me how to create opportunities for my students to experience success. Thank You that You did not give up on me but created multiple opportunities for me to hear Your Word and receive You. Help me to model Your love and behavior in my classroom creating many opportunities for my students to learn and be successful. When they do not master concepts the first time, help me to never give up on them like You never gave up on me.

In Jesus' Name
Amen

Day 45 Strong & Courageous

Be strong and of good courage, do not fear nor be afraid of them;
for the LORD your God He is the One who goes with you.
He will never leave you or forsake you. Deuteronomy 31:6

CONGRATULATIONS! YOU HAVE REACHED THE halfway point of
the semester, and you are to be commended for this significant
achievement. Take a moment to acknowledge the influence you
have had on your students and the positive learning environment
you have created. Throughout the Bible, God admonishes believers to be strong and courageous. Being strong and courageous
means trusting in the Lord as your true source of strength. The
Lord, your God, walks beside you every step of the way, offering
strength, courage, and a source of unwavering support. These
words are comforting because if God is for you, the victory is
secure. The forces of heaven are backing you as you teach God's
children. As you continue the journey as an educator, remember
that you are never alone. No matter the challenges you are facing today, be strong and courageous. Hold your head up, walk
confidently, and stand firmly on the promises of God's Word,
knowing that He will never leave you or forsake you. Cast all
your cares upon Him, and He will carry these burdens for you.

Declare your need for Him, and express gratitude for His guidance in every aspect of your teaching journey. Psalm 138:8 is a reminder that the Lord will perfect that which concerns you. May the second half of the semester be filled with continued strength, courage, and moments of profound impact on your students. Your dedication to shaping young minds is commendable, and I am confident that your influence will endure throughout the remainder of the school year.

Abba,

Thank You for Your command to be strong and courageous. I will not fear the challenges that are before me this week. I know that You are on my side and that You are fighting for me. I know that no matter what happens You can cause every negative situation to work for my good. I thank You that You have not given me a spirit of fear. I walk into my school and my classroom confidently today knowing that You are with me, and You have promised to never leave me or forsake me.

In Jesus' Name
Amen

Day 46 Nurturing the Mind & Spirit

It is written, Man shall not live by bread alone, but by every word that proceedeth out of the mouth of God. Matthew 4:4

TODAY'S SCRIPTURE IS A REMINDER that you cannot live without the nourishment of God's Word. Take a moment to reflect on these words of Jesus within the context of your teaching journey. You are called to nourish not only the minds but also the spirits of those entrusted to your care. Just as physical nourishment is needed for survival, the words you share, the wisdom you impart, and the values you instill contribute to the holistic development of your students. Your commitment to instilling values, fostering critical thinking, nurturing character, and developing essential soft skills is a powerful testament to the magic that happens within the realm of education. It's not just a job; it's a calling that you embrace with passion and purpose. Your classroom is not just a space for learning but a community where young people develop and grow on the journey of life. This is evident when you witness students supporting one another, and forming friendships that extend beyond the walls of the classroom. These are the moments that breathe life into the educational experience, turning it into a thrilling journey. You are not just creating academically skilled individuals, but you are also nurturing future problem solvers preparing them to be productive citizens. When it is time to award students for their accomplishments, remember the accomplishments that are not necessarily tangible like awards for teamwork, collaboration, and citizenship. Your commitment to creating a classroom that values not only academic achievement but also personal growth is an inspiration for young people seeking to understand themselves and their place in the world. You are a guide, a mentor, and a source of wisdom, contributing to the spiritual and intellectual nourishment of those who look up to you.

Abba,

Your Word is a lamp unto my feet and a light unto my path. Give me a hunger and a desire for Your Word. Thank You for Your Word that tells us that I cannot survive off bread alone. Show me how to nurture the hearts, minds, and souls of the students under my care. Help me to remember that my role is not just imparting information but modeling skills that are important in the world. Thank You for Jesus' example of regularly spending time in Your Word. Show me how to follow Jesus' example.

In Jesus' Name
Amen

Day 47 Building a Caring Community

Be kindly affectioned one to another with brotherly love;
in honour preferring one another. Romans 12:10

THIS VERSE REFLECTS THE KIND of supportive and inclusive community needed in a school environment. It calls us to embrace love, treating each other with kindness, respect, and genuine devotion in a spirit of unity. Unity in the classroom, grade level, and school is imperative. There can only be true unity when everyone is working together toward common goals. You can model unity by being a team player and working cooperatively with your team. In the pursuit of unity, avoid selfish ambition and instead be willing to yield to the ideas and suggestions of others. Remember, Jesus is your standard and model. Honor everyone at your school, including the students, cafeteria staff, custodians, and office staff. Treating everyone fairly is a cornerstone of the commitment to brotherly love. The custodians, as integral members of your school family, deserve the same honor and respect as the superintendent. Intentionally recognizing and respecting everyone is crucial. Avoiding favoritism among students and promoting empathy and compassion contribute to high school morale. Encourage students to show empathy and compassion towards their peers and proactively address any form of bullying or negative behavior. The implementation of conflict resolution strategies and the promotion of positive communication further contribute to creating a healthy and nurturing learning environment. Be a part of the solution and not a part of the problems at your school. Remember the children are watching and you are modeling the love of Christ. Your commitment to fostering unity, inclusion, and brotherly love is instrumental in creating a positive and transformative school environment.

Abba,

Thank You for this day. Thank you that you love each of us, and you are no respecter of persons. I trust You with every aspect of my life. Thank You for my coworkers and colleagues. Help me to be a blessing to the people in my grade and in my school. I set my eyes on You, and I focus on my assignment. I work cooperatively with my coworkers and not in a spirit of competition. Help me to always be willing to show honor to others regardless of their position or titles. When I go into my classroom, I remember that You are my God and my portion forever.

In Jesus' Name
Amen

Day 48 Intentional Inclusion

He predestined us for adoption to sonship through Jesus Christ,
in accordance with his pleasure and will.
Ephesians 1:5 (NIV)

GOD INTENTIONALLY SENT HIS SON to save the entire world. Just as God values the entire world, you can recognize and honor the individuality of each student in your classroom. By embracing different backgrounds and cultures, you can create an environment where every student feels valued and accepted. Take the time to get to know each student individually. Learn about their interests, backgrounds, and personal experiences. This can be done through surveys, one-on-one conversations, or icebreaker activities. Create or volunteer to serve on your school's Multicultural or Diversity Committee. Just as God's plan for salvation encompasses the entire world, the intentional embrace of diverse cultures reflects a commitment to God's plan of unity in Christ. In the Sumter County School District, the Japanese Exchange program was a valuable initiative to expose students to different cultures and instill a sense of acceptance. Middle and high school students would embark on a week-long trip to experience the diverse culture of the host school. During a specific year, I had the privilege of serving as the principal and as a host family. The initial days of the program were filled with cultural exchanges, sharing traditions, language, and daily experiences. In a culminating event, the Japanese students performed traditional dances and shared parting gifts. Reflecting on this exchange program, I witnessed the powerful impact of intentional inclusivity. The school became an example of God's adoption plan, where every student felt chosen, valued, and accepted for who they were. The experience confirmed the benefits of recognizing and celebrating the individuality and cultural diversity of each student. You can confirm the divine intentionality of God's love for the world by celebrating and honoring all cultures represented in your classroom and school.

Abba,

I praise You for Your goodness to me. Thank You that through the blood of Jesus, You have adopted me into Your family. Thank You that You have called me by name, and I know who I am in You. I submit myself to Your divine authority. Be with me as I interact with the children and adults in my school. I remember that I wrestle not against flesh and blood but against wickedness in heavenly places. Thank You that You have given Your angels charge over me. Equip me to respond to everyone in a manner that pleases You.

In Jesus' Name
Amen

Day 49 Embracing the Journey Ahead

Brethren, I count not myself to have apprehended: but this one thing I do, forgetting those things which are behind, and reaching forth unto those things which are before, I press toward the mark for the prize of the high calling of God in Christ Jesus. 3:13-14

TODAY'S SCRIPTURE URGES BELIEVERS NOT to focus on the past, but on the unlimited possibilities that lie ahead. This forward focus will require you to approach each new day with a fresh perspective, unburdened by the challenges of yesterday. It's natural to find yourself dwelling on the past, replaying lessons, interactions, or challenges that didn't go as planned. However, this scripture is an encouragement to press forward, leaving behind past mistakes and distractions. By choosing to forget those things that are behind you, you free yourself to focus on the potential for the future. When these past thoughts invade your thoughts, make the intentional choice to forgive and forget. Forgiveness and letting go of past grievances, whether big or small, are crucial to creating an environment conducive to learning and inspiration. Each day offers a fresh opportunity to make a lasting impact on the lives entrusted to your care. A similar scripture, found in Isaiah 43:18-19 (NIV), echoes this sentiment: "Forget the former things; do not dwell on the past. See, I am doing a new thing! Now it springs up; do you not perceive it? I am making a way in the wilderness and streams in the wasteland." As you continue this semester, forget the challenges of yesterday. Rather than viewing them as hindrances, perceive them as opportunities for reflection, learning, and advancement. "Forgetting those things which are behind," means you cannot look back at past mistakes, failures, temptations, or anything that distracts you from focusing on "the upward call of God in Christ."

Abba,

Thank You for this day. I set my eyes on Jesus, The Author and The Finisher of my faith. Help me to consciously capture any negative thoughts of the past taking up space in my mind. I capture those thoughts and bring them into submission and the obedience of Christ. I choose to forget past mistakes, hurts, and memories that hinder me from moving forward with You. Thank You that You will never leave me or forsake me. Thank You that You are with me facing the challenges of each day with me. I thank You for Your Son, Jesus, and the gift of Your Holy Spirit. I draw on Your strength to face another day and every challenge ahead of me.

In Jesus' Name
Amen

Day 50 Quenching the Thirst

Jesus answered her, if you knewest the gift of God, and who it is that saith to you, give me to drink; thou wouldest have asked Him, and He would have given thee living water John 4:10

JESUS' WORDS TO THE WOMAN at the well are a reminder that the answer to spiritual thirst lies in seeking Him – the Well of Living Water. Just as Jesus offered living water to the woman at the well, as an educator, you can provide students with an enriching and emotionally satisfying learning experience. Many students come to school in search of love, support, understanding, and a source of inspiration. Students also need emotional satisfaction, a sense of belonging, and a supportive environment to thrive. By fostering a positive and inclusive classroom, you contribute to their overall development, addressing not only their academic needs but also their emotional well-being. During my years as Principal of Staley Middle School, Counselor Daphene Williams coordinated a Mentor Program that paired students in need of emotional support with teacher mentors. The school leaders and teaching staff embraced this initiative, collaborating to offer unwavering support, encouragement, and resources to the identified students. I had the privilege of participating in this program as a mentor to a remarkable student named Kanijah. Together, we worked with community organizations to ensure students like Kanijah had access to essentials such as school supplies, nourishment, and crucial emotional support. This Mentor Program served not only as a lifeline for students but also as a catalyst for their academic success. It exemplified the power of creating a network of support, much like living water, extending beyond the classroom. Commit to creating an environment where this living water flows freely. In doing so, you become a vessel of inspiration that empowers your students to flourish intellectually, emotionally, and spiritually.

Abba,

I praise You that You are the Well of Living Water. You refresh my soul. Forgive me for looking for fulfillment in other places when You are all that I need. I come to abide in You and I know that apart from You I can do nothing. I ask for Your help, guidance, and direction to teach Your children. I trust that You are with me and will help me through every challenge that I face. I thank You for sending Jesus to take my place. I allow You to fill my longing heart so that I can bring light and joy to others around me. I decrease and I allow You to increase in my life. Thank You for the satisfaction that is only found in Your presence. May Your will be done in my life.

In Jesus' Name
Amen

Day 51 Guided by Faith

Trust in the LORD with all your heart, And lean not on your own understanding. In all thy ways acknowledge Him, and He shall direct thy paths. Proverbs 3:5-6

TEACHING IS A JOURNEY FILLED with diverse challenges and joys. It is natural to encounter situations where your understanding may fall short, and uncertainties may arise. However, today's scripture from the book of Proverbs encourages believers to place their trust wholeheartedly in the Lord. In moments of doubt or when faced with the unexpected, lean on His wisdom, knowing that your reliance on Him surpasses all earthly understanding. The scripture invites you to acknowledge God in all your ways. In the planning of lessons, the interactions with students, and the collaborative efforts with colleagues, purposefully acknowledge the divine guidance of God. As you acknowledge and entrust your endeavors to Him, you open yourself to His direction, finding assurance in His ability to lead you on your teaching journey. Human minds cannot fathom the vastness of The Creator, whose ways and thoughts transcend understanding. Spending consistent time in prayer offers you a clear picture of how big God is and reminds believers of His sovereignty. Mrs. Rutine Mathis, a respected educator, and friend, eloquently recounts a story illustrating how God used a humble 1st-grade student to offer her words of encouragement precisely when she needed them. The student's simple, yet profound, words penetrated Mrs. Rutine's heart. It was a timely reminder that, in the vastness of God's plan, even the smallest voices can carry the weight of divine encouragement. Leaning not to your understanding is knowing that God has many ways to communicate to you – even using a little kid. As you trust in the Lord with all your heart, you pave the way for divine interactions and direction. Allow today's scripture to be a source of strength, assurance, and unwavering trust as you navigate the rewarding yet challenging path of education.

Abba,

I praise You because You are wonderful in counsel and excellent in wisdom. I trust You with all of my heart and I lean not to my understanding today. I thank You for my job and the opportunity to influence Your children each day. I know that You are the answer to the stressful demands of teaching children. I come to enjoy the refreshing presence of Your Spirit. In Your presence, there is fullness of joy and in Your right hand, there are pleasures forever more. I come boldly to Your throne to receive the grace and mercy that I need. I confess that I cannot do this job without You. You are the sovereign God of the universe, and You know what is best for me. I put my trust in You today.

In Jesus' Name
Amen

Day 52 Take Your Cross

And he that taketh not his cross and followeth after Me, is not worthy of Me. Matthew 10:38

PAUSE, BREATHE, AND REFLECT ON the commitment and sacrifice that comes with following Christ. As an educator, you are called to carry your cross—the challenges, responsibilities, and sacrifices that are part of the profession. Each day presents a new opportunity to make a difference in students' lives, but it also brings its share of trials. Just as Christ bore His cross for the greater good, educators carry a cross in the pursuit of shaping young minds and nurturing the leaders of tomorrow. Jesus' sacrifice led to salvation and your commitment to education impacts lives and shapes futures. It is in the long hours of lesson planning, the dedication to each student's growth, and the selfless acts that often go unnoticed that you find the essence of your calling. Even in moments when the load feels heavy, remember that, with Christ as your guide, you are equipped to carry the cross with resilience, determination, and an enduring sense of purpose. Keep pressing forward, for in your commitment to education, you reflect the profound love and sacrifice modeled by Jesus. You are unknowingly crafting a legacy that will extend far beyond the classroom, influencing generations to come. As you continue this journey, may you find strength and inspiration to know that your impact is immeasurable and that your commitment reflects the very essence of God's unfailing love. Because your role is vital, embrace each day with the assurance that, just as Christ found joy in His sacrifice, your commitment to education is a path to the joy of shaping minds and impacting lives.

Abba,

Thank You for this day. I come to surrender my life to You today. I am no longer living for myself, but I take up my cross to follow Your plans for my life. Thank You for Jesus' example. For the joy that was set before Him, He endured the cross. I don't look for approval from people, but my goal is to please You. Thank You that You have chosen and appointed me to teach Your children. I accept Your call for my life. I thank You that You are with me and will never leave me or forsake me. You stand with me as I fulfill Your purpose for my life. I stand on the promises of Your Word. May Your will be done in my life.

In Jesus' Name
Amen

Day 53 The Lord is On Your Side

The LORD is on my side; I will not fear. What (mere) can man do unto me? The LORD is on my side, He is among those who help me... Psalm 118:6

TEACHING IS A CALLING THAT requires perseverance, dedication, and a compassionate heart. There will be moments when the weight of responsibilities feels heavy, and the pressures may attempt to cast doubt on your purpose. It is during these times that you must cling to the powerful truth that the Lord is on your side. Fear, doubt, and anxiety may knock at the door of your heart, but you can boldly declare, "I will not fear." The Lord, your Helper, is present in your classroom, guiding your efforts and providing the wisdom needed to nurture young minds. With the Almighty by your side, there is an assurance that you can overcome any challenges that come your way. God has the power to prevent, counteract, or turn every situation for your ultimate good. Teachers often allow external pressures like the evaluation process, testing, and accountability to frustrate them. Do not allow these distractions to shift your focus from the core calling of shaping young minds and fostering a love for learning. It is essential to remember that while administrative demands are a part of the profession, they do not overshadow your dedication to the growth and development of each student. Keep the flame of your passion burning bright, because it is this commitment that overcomes the temporary obstacles in the educational journey. As you embark on this school day, carry with you the truth that the Lord is there to help you. Seek His guidance in your endeavors, find peace in His promises, and teach with the confidence that comes from knowing you are not alone. With the Lord by your side, you can face every challenge, shape every mind, and make a lasting impact on the future.

Abba,

Thank You that You are on my side and causing all things to work for my good. I will not fear what people can do to me. I humble myself under Your mighty hand today. I thank You that You have given me the victory and called me an overcomer. You are with me and I know you will never leave me or forsake me. I can do all things through Christ who strengthens me. No weapon that is formed against me will prosper. You have given Your angels charge over me. I choose to keep my mind on You knowing You will keep me in perfect peace.

In Jesus' Name
Amen

Day 54 Set the Atmosphere

Fathers, provoke not Your children to anger, lest they be discouraged. Colossians 3:21

ALTHOUGH DIRECTED TO PARENTS, TODAY'S scripture can certainly apply to teachers. Teachers can easily provoke children and cause them to become discouraged. Teachers can inadvertently provoke students through subtle ways like using sarcasm, making comparisons, and setting unrealistic expectations. These seemingly minor behaviors can have a significant impact, creating an atmosphere that discourages rather than motivates. It is important that you self-reflect and watch your tone with students. Each child is different, and some are sensitive to a harsh tone and feelings of disrespect. Your words have the power to discourage and provoke children. Because you don't know what children are dealing with in their home environments, you must be careful with words of correction. Never use sarcasm with students or say things that could embarrass a child in front of peers. Do your best to not engage in power struggles with students. Seek ways to make your commands respectful, showing that you have high expectations, and you expect compliance to requests. In instances where students exhibit behaviors tolerated at home but are unacceptable in the school environment, the emphasis should be on gentle reminders rather than criticism or judgment. Ignoring negative behavior whenever possible and actively recognizing positive behaviors creates a more constructive classroom environment. Give students what is just and fair, knowing that you also have a master in heaven (Colossians 4:8). By being mindful of tone, choosing words carefully, and approaching situations with empathy, teachers can create an environment where students feel supported, encouraged, and empowered to learn and grow. This aligns with the scripture's call to parents (and by extension, teachers) to avoid provoking children and instead, guide them with kindness and understanding.

Abba,

Thank You for the education profession. Thank You for the opportunity to influence and be a model for Your children. Help me to not allow any unwholesome communication to come out of my mouth but good words that edify. Forgive me for the times that I have missed the mark in this area. Let me not be controlled by my emotions to respond negatively when students are non-compliant. Help me to train them in the way that they should go. Give me the grace to remain calm and see past negative student behaviors. I set the tone and the atmosphere for my classroom.

In Jesus' Name
Amen

Day 55 Embracing Grace

Dearly beloved, avenge not yourselves, but rather give place unto wrath: for it is written, Vengeance is mine; I will repay, saith the Lord. Romans 12:19

THIS PASSAGE FROM THE BOOK of Romans is as a gentle reminder that in the face of adversity, we are called to embrace grace and relinquish desires for vengeance or revenge. Teaching requires a heart attuned to compassion and forgiveness. Classroom dynamics can be difficult to navigate, and it's not uncommon for conflicts to arise. However, as an educator, you are encouraged to rise above the instinct for retaliation. Instead, create spaces where forgiveness, understanding, and grace prevail. It is natural to desire a form of justice when faced with perceived wrongs, but the Scripture invites us to trust in the divine order of things. "Vengeance is mine; I will repay, saith the Lord" speaks to the overarching theme of surrendering our grievances to God, trusting that a just resolution will be certain. After a conflict with students, parents, or coworkers, be the first to display forgiveness by not walking in offense and by keeping the lines of communication open. While this does not always mean that you continue to interact with the person at the same level, you must however choose to walk in forgiveness. "Repay no one evil for evil" (Romans 12:17) and "overcome evil with good" (Romans 12: 21) are the instructions from God's word. With students, be intentional to communicate that each day is a fresh start. Keeping the lines of communication open with parents will indicate that you do not walk in revenge. If you are tempted in this area, remind yourself that God will repay. His vengeance always flows from a place of justice, not a place of revenge. Rest assured that when people have wronged you, justice will come. Be not deceived; God is not mocked: for whatsoever a man soweth, that shall he also reap (Galatians 6:7). By embodying these virtues, you not only model a profound life lesson for your students but also contribute to a positive and harmonious educational environment.

Abba,

You are the Lord who makes all things and stretches out the heavens (Isiah 44:24 NIV). I come to abide in You knowing that apart from You I can do nothing. I cannot teach Your children without You. I ask for Your help, guidance, and direction as I move throughout the day. I trust that You are with me and will help me through every challenge that I face. I declare that vengeance is Yours. I allow You to repay any offense or evil towards me. I know that You cause everyone to reap what they sow. Help me to sow good seeds. May Your will be done in my life.

In Jesus' Name
Amen

Day 56 *Generosity Rewarded*

Give, and it shall be given to you; good measure, pressed down, and shaken together, and running over, shall men give into your bosom. Luke 6:38

As a teacher, you are daily engaged in the acts of giving – giving knowledge, guidance, support, and, most importantly, love to your students. This act of giving, according to our scriptural reference today, is not in vain but is a force that creates a ripple effect. Most teachers are natural givers and constantly spend their own money to create a welcoming classroom environment. In the ongoing talk about teacher pay, it is impressive to see teachers, despite limited funds, generously helping their students. Teachers buy gifts during holidays, treats for good behavior, and often help students in need personally. Many schools collaborate to collectively support a child or family in need during the holiday seasons. I remember the annual Bobcat Coat Drive led by Mrs. Wanda Miles during my tenure in The Dooly County School System. The initiative involved collaboration with local businesses, community members, and school staff. Donations poured in, ranging from new coats and jackets to hats and gloves. Seeing the smiles on students' faces as they received these essential winter items is something I will never forget. Even when resources are limited, if you put the needs of others first, God somehow finds ways to meet your own needs. Pray and ask God for creative ideas to support students in need, and trust Him to reward you. When you give to the least of these - your students - God has promised that He will reward you (Matthew 25:40). The Bible says that He who gives to the poor loans to God (Proverbs 19:17). As you continue to invest in the lives of your students, remember that the more you give, the more you receive.

Abba,

Thank You that the Earth is Yours and everything in it belongs to You. You are the sovereign God of the universe. I surrender my money and my resources to You. Thank You for providing for all of my needs. Your eye is on the sparrow, and I trust that You will take care of me. You desire above all things that I should prosper and be in good health. Thank You that You loved the world so much that You gave Your Son. Help me to give selflessly to others, knowing that You are my source and my provider. I thank You that Your goodness and mercy will follow me all the days of my life and I will dwell in Your house forever.

In Jesus' Name
Amen

Day 57 Divine Calling

For we are His workmanship, created in Christ Jesus unto good works, which God hath before ordained that we should walk in them. Ephesians 2:10

YOU ARE AN ESSENTIAL PART of God's grand design, equipped with unique talents to fulfill His good works. Every lesson you teach, every encouraging word you share, and every moment of guidance contributes to the larger plan that God has laid out. Your labor is not in vain, and through your commitment to education, you are actively participating in the fulfillment of God's purpose for the lives of your students. Like the Prophet Jeremiah, before God formed you in the womb, He knew you and set you apart for His purposes (Jeremiah 1:5). Do not underestimate the influence that you have over the students at your school. Each day is not a random occurrence, but a part of a well-crafted plan recorded in His book. Revelation 4:11 is a reminder that you were created and exist for His good pleasure, and despite any perceived imperfections, God, the Potter, has not made any mistakes in forming you. As you meditate on His goodness, remember that every student who sits in your classroom was uniquely created by Him. Find ways to validate and affirm each student.

Verbally communicate your belief in each student's potential and ability to succeed. When students are struggling, provide words of assurance that you believe they will master the skills and provide opportunities for reteaching and remediation. Encourage students to set high expectations for themselves and support them in reaching those goals. Rest assured that God, in His omniscience, prepared you for this moment. Just as Esther was chosen for a specific purpose (Esther 4:14), recognize that you have also been appointed for such a time as this to fulfill His divine will. Find strength in the assurance that God is with you in this very moment.

Abba,

You are The Potter, and I am the clay. Thank You for creating me for good works in You before the foundation of the world. Thank You for choosing me to work with Your children. I accept Your high calling for my life. Today, I choose to walk in Your ways and accept Your peace and contentment for my journey. I decrease so that You can increase in me. I let go of all distractions and issues that would cause me to keep from focusing on You. You are the Well of Living Water. Thank You for the refreshment that is found only in Your presence. Thank You that nothing can separate me from Your love that is in Christ Jesus. May each of my students feel Your love through me.

In Jesus' Name
Amen

Day 58 Lasting Impact

Be kind to one another; tenderhearted, forgiving one another, just as God in Christ also forgave you. Ephesians 4:32

I HAVE FOND MEMORIES OF many of my former teachers, especially the ones who instilled in me a love for learning and belief in my potential. A teacher's goal should be for students to remember them in a similar light— as someone who goes beyond just teaching, fostering a passion for learning and building confidence in their abilities. Living in the close-knit community of Americus, GA, I frequently run into former students who have become successful business owners, esteemed professionals, and valued community members. Even though many years have passed, they remember me, and it is fulfilling to know I played a part, no matter how small, in their success. Because your students will one day be adults who remember you, today's verse is a reminder to be kind, tenderhearted, and forgiving. You are called to model the love of Christ, not based on someone's behavior towards you, but on Christ's behavior towards you. Every day, strive to offer your students and coworkers a clean slate, fostering an environment of grace and understanding. Many of my former students have become authors, and their achievements motivate and inspire me on my journey. Highlighting the mutual exchange in our teacher-student relationship, my former student Travis Rush, now an author and entrepreneur, has provided me with great business advice. Another former student Maya Tyson is currently my stylist and beautician. Never underestimate the future potential of your current students. Considering the lasting impact you will have as a teacher; today's scripture stresses the importance of kindness and forgiveness. Aim to model Christ's love by offering a clean slate each day, promoting a forgiving and understanding atmosphere among your students and colleagues.

Abba,

You are the Well of Living Water. I come praising You for Your goodness to me. I acknowledge Your presence with me today. I surrender to Your will in my classroom and my school. I know that You are leading me and guiding me throughout the day. Help me to listen to and obey the voice of Your Spirit. Help me to walk in peace, love, and forgiveness with everyone I encounter. I forgive my students and coworkers for any offense. You have a divine plan for each of my students and You are using me to execute Your master plan. I thank You for Jesus' model of love and forgiveness.

In Jesus' Name
Amen

Day 59 Stepping Out of the Boat

So He said, "Come." And when Peter had come down out of the boat, he walked on the water to go to Jesus. Matthew 14:29 (NKJV)

THE IDEA THAT TEACHING IS a "superpower" is often used to emphasize the profound and life-changing impact of the profession. In today's scripture, Peter accomplishes the seemingly impossible act of stepping out of a boat and walking on water. When Peter saw Jesus on the water, he asked to join Him and briefly had the faith to do the impossible. Peter could have remained in the boat with the other disciples. The boat symbolizes the comfort of routine and familiarity, but the call to greatness is outside the boat. Stepping out of the boat requires courage, faith, and a willingness to embrace the extraordinary. It took much faith for Peter to walk on water, even if it was just for a moment. Similarly, Jesus invites you to rise above the ordinary and step out of your comfort zone. To get out of the boat, be determined to follow Jesus, be ready to take risks, and embrace new approaches. Be willing to take risks and try new innovative practices, moving away from traditional methods. Just as Jesus prevented Peter from sinking, He promises to support you as well. It is humbling to imagine

Jesus reaching into the water to save Peter. A similar scripture from Isaiah 43:2 reassures that when you pass through challenges, He will be with you, ensuring you will not be overwhelmed. Be willing to follow Jesus and step out of the familiar "boat" of traditional teaching methods and navigate new waters, providing students with a richer and more impactful learning experience. Embracing this call requires not just faith but a bold willingness to innovate and navigate new territories, ensuring that education becomes transformative in the lives of your students.

Abba,

Thank You for a new day and a new opportunity to stand in front of Your children and teach them new concepts. Thank You for the new adventures for today. I face this day with excitement knowing that You are with me. I surrender my will to Your will today. I put my faith in You today. I surrender to Your desire to do something new and different through me with Your students. Show me how to choose to listen to Your voice daily and beckon me to get out of the boat and do the impossible with You. Thank You that with You there is nothing impossible. I keep my eyes on You and You will keep me in perfect peace.

In Jesus' Name
Amen

Day 60 Unwavering Faith

Therefore, my beloved brethren, be ye steadfast, unmoveable, always abounding in the work of the Lord, forasmuch as ye know that your labour is not in vain in the Lord.
1 Corinthians 15:58

WHEN APPLIED TO YOUR ROLES as a teacher, today's scripture encourages you to be steadfast and unmovable in your commitment to believing in every child's ability to learn. Approach each day with unwavering faith in each student's ability to learn, grow, and excel. Remember that every child is a work in progress, and your faith in their potential can be a source of encouragement. Be the force that pushes them to reach new heights, to overcome challenges, and to believe in themselves. Do not allow students to accept failure as an option. Your faith in their abilities can be the catalyst that propels them toward success. Robyn Jackson, author of *"Never Work Harder than Your Students & Other Principles of Great Teaching"* (2nd Edition), shares that educators must maintain unwavering faith believing that they can succeed with the most challenging students even in the face of repeated failure. She encourages educators to not give up quickly but to persist until a measure of success is achieved. Jackson encourages teachers to find time during the school day (at lunch, after school, recess) for students to complete required assignments. This unwavering faith can be powerfully reassuring to students, especially those with a history of failure. Your role is not just to teach but to cultivate an environment where students reach their full potential. High expectations insist that every student gives their best effort and provides the necessary support for success. May your dedication continue to sow seeds of success in the hearts and minds of your students.

Abba,

I praise You that You are the Most High God. I have come to acknowledge that there is none greater and none stronger. I submit myself to Your divine authority today. Thank You for the redemptive work of Jesus that gives me access to You. I set my affection and attention on You. I invite You into every detail of my classroom. Help me to teach as unto You and not for my principal or school leaders because You are my reward. I lift my students and their parents to You. I lift my school leaders to You. May Your will be done in my life today.

In Jesus' Name
Amen

Day 61 Navigating the Storms

Behold, God is my salvation; I will trust and not be afraid:
for the LORD Jehovah is my strength and my song;
He also is become my salvation. Isaiah 12:2

CHALLENGES ARE AN INEVITABLE PART of the teaching journey. Navigating the storms involves placing trust in God, who is your strength during difficult times. Instead of allowing temporary storms to cause you to reconsider your career choice, allow them to become stepping stones for continued success. The key to weathering storms is to anchor yourself in unwavering faith in your calling and purpose. There will be days when the most well-behaved students exhibit frustrating behaviors, and lessons don't go as planned. See challenges as opportunities for growth and learning, trusting that they build strength and resilience. In her book, *From Burnt Out to Fired Up: Reigniting Your Passion for Teaching (2022)*, Morgane Michael shares exercises that educators can use to overcome perfectionism, improve internal self-talk, and reduce stress by reframing their mindset. Michael further encourages educators to develop "toxic positivity" by always aiming to see the bright side of every struggle as an educator. Keeping an attitude of gratitude and remaining focused on your purpose will also sustain you during difficult days. Remember you are leaving a lasting impact on your students. You are also encouraged to connect with fellow teachers or trusted mentors for support on difficult days. Share concerns and challenges and allow others to provide encouragement and a different perspective. God has your back and will guide you through any challenge; all you need to do is have faith. The storm will pass, and troubles are temporary. Drawing inspiration from Psalm 30:5, weeping may endure for a night, but joy comes in the morning. Keep the faith and remember that the battle belongs to the Lord.

Abba,

I come to praise You because You are the sovereign God of the universe. You have said that if I keep my mind stayed on You, You will keep me in perfect peace. I thank You that You have ultimate power over the storms I face. I set my focus and attention on You knowing that You are my refuge and my strength. You are a very present help in the times of trouble. I trust You when things go well, and I trust You during the storms. Thank You for providing peace that passes all understanding. I thank You that You are causing all things to work together for the good.

In Jesus' Name
Amen

Day 62 Tame the Tongue

The tongue is a fire, a world of iniquity: so is the tongue among our members, that it defileth the whole body, and setteth on fire the course of nature; and it is set on fire of hell. James 3:6

IN THE PURSUIT OF CREATING an environment conducive to learning, educators occasionally guide students to quiet down or hush. Honestly, you know there is nothing worse than that class full of talkative students or that one student who talks excessively. Educators must heed their own advice and practice being quiet or hushing when necessary. Today's scripture serves as a reminder of the potential danger of unchecked words. James further tells us that we should be slow to speak and quick to listen (James 1:19). Many people (educators, too) can be found talking too much about the wrong things. Educators must recognize the potential repercussions of their words, acknowledging the role they play in shaping not only the learning environment but also the future aspirations of students. As you mature in The Word and grow closer to God, you must learn to tame your tongue. Silence is often the wisest choice when you have nothing positive to contribute. James vividly describes the tongue as a potential source of fire and evil. Choosing silence when negativity arises is an act of wisdom, allowing space for constructive thoughts and intentional speech. It is essential to break the habit of complaining about students, the school, or its leaders. Unfortunately, negative words have led to many people not choosing the career as an educator that God has ordained for them. The Bible says so much about the power of our words. Monitoring your thoughts and intentionally focusing on the positive aspects of your profession, students, and school is crucial. Turn to prayer to express frustrations and avoid becoming entangled in the trap of spreading or listening to school gossip. Life and death are in the power of the tongue.

Abba,

I bless You for Your goodness to me. Thank You for the education profession. Help me to allow no unwholesome communication to come out of my mouth but words that edify and bring grace. Help me to learn to tame my tongue and keep my mouth closed when I have nothing good to say. Let me not be controlled by my emotions to respond negatively when things do not go my way. Help me to intentionally share the good that is happening in my classroom and my school. Help me to see the good and be a champion for the education profession. Help me to be slow to speak and quick to listen. I know that I will give an account for every idle word that I have spoken.

In Jesus' Name
Amen

Day 63 Joy in the Journey

Be not ye therefore like unto them: for your Father knoweth what things ye have need of before ye ask Him. Matthew 6:8

TEACHING IS FUN AND BRINGS joy with each new day. The delight in witnessing the "light bulb" moments of young minds and the growth of students at the end of the year adds a special dimension to the profession. Finding joy in teaching involves developing a mindset of focusing on the positive aspects of teaching and allowing these moments to overshadow the challenges. Taking the time to savor the job and appreciate the students contributes to a positive and enjoyable teaching experience. Amidst lesson plans, grading, and other responsibilities, remember to appreciate the moments of joy in your day. View each day as a journey led by God. Seek ways to not only find joy within yourself but also to allow it to spill over and illuminate the learning experiences of your students. In Eric Jensen's book, *"Poor Students, Rich Teaching,"* he explores ways educators can foster "eudaimonic happiness" in students, a type of joy that significantly impacts the emotional well-being of students facing poverty and chronic stress. Jensen suggests strategic approaches such as assigning culminating projects, sharing exemplary work, and utilizing positive reinforcement techniques. These positive reinforcers include simple gestures like smiles, affirmations, written feedback, and positive notes sent home to parents. According to Jensen, these strategies indirectly improve academic achievement and create a positive learning environment. In these final weeks of the semester, savor the joyous moments that come your way. Whether it's sharing a laugh with students, experiencing the satisfaction of a well-executed lesson, or enjoying the camaraderie of a supportive colleague, these moments contribute to the overall en"joy"ment of your teaching experience. Take the time to be grateful for the aspects of the job that you love, and never lose sight of why you accepted the challenge to teach. After all, the beauty of teaching lies not in the destination but in the journey itself.

Abba,

Thank You for life, health, and strength. Thank You that Your Word says that You daily load me with benefits (Psalm 68:19). I thank You for being a good Father to me. You are perfect in all Your ways, and You have not made any mistakes concerning me. You know my end from my beginning, and You have ordained this day for me. Forgive me for trying to carry the heavy load of teaching my students and independent of You. I take the time to cast all my cares upon You because You care for me. Help me to enjoy the abundant life that Jesus came for me to enjoy. Show me how to relax and enjoy teaching Your children.

In Jesus' Name
Amen

Day 64 Cultivating Contentment

Not that I speak in respect of want: for I have learned in whatsoever state I am in, therewith be content. Philippians 4:11

WHEN DO TEACHERS EXPERIENCE A sense of contentment? Contrary to popular belief, contentment for educators can be found not only during summer vacation but also in the day-to-day experiences of teaching. Perhaps you feel content when witnessing a struggling student finally grasp a challenging concept or observing student growth from the beginning to the end of the school year. Witnessing former students excel in life and knowing you played a part in their journey also brings a profound sense of fulfillment. In today's scripture, Paul shares from prison that regardless of his circumstances, he had "learned" to be content. Similarly, educators can also "learn" to be content despite challenges or circumstances. You "learn" contentment by knowing that the work you do is meaningful and that you are making a difference. Contentment in teaching means appreciating the small wins each day and realizing the lasting impact you have on students. Recognize that each lesson and every challenge overcome contributes to a brighter future for your students. To find contentment in teaching, you should also appreciate the unique

126

qualities of each student and trust that even during difficult times, everything will work together for good. Jesus desires for you to live a life of joy, happiness, and contentment. As 1 Timothy 6:6 beautifully expresses, "But godliness with contentment is great gain." We brought nothing into the world, and we cannot take anything out." Cultivate contentment by embracing the joy of teaching, and by recognizing that teaching makes all other professions possible. No matter what you are facing or how you are feeling today, know that you are making a difference.

Abba,

Thank You that You have the whole world in Your hands. Thank You that this world is not my home and that I am a Kingdom citizen. I choose to set my affections and my hope on You. Help me to learn to be content in whatever circumstances You allow in my life. Forgive me for the lust of the flesh, the lust of the eye, and the pride of life (1 John 2:16). Help me always remember that this world is passing away but whoever does the will of God lives forever. I decrease myself today and allow You to continue to shape me and mold me into the image of my dear Savior. Thank you that you are on my side and causing things to work together for my good.

In Jesus' Name
Amen

Day 65 Gratitude

In everything give thanks: for this is the will of God in Christ Jesus concerning you. 1 Thessalonians 5:18

GRATITUDE, ESPECIALLY IN ADVERSITY, IS a discipline that can transform your perspective and align your heart with God's purposes for your life. You must train yourself to thank God for everything. Yes, everything. Disciplining yourself to express gratitude, even in the face of difficulties, is an essential practice. It involves thanking God for both the good and the challenging days of your journey. Constantly focusing on the difficulties of the job leads to a negative mindset and potential burnout. However, it is through the lens of gratitude that you take control and align yourself with the divine will of God. Decide that you will remain positive even on your difficult days and make the joy of the Lord your strength. A joyful heart is not subject to the circumstances around you. To foster this positive mindset, consider reflecting on three things you are grateful for in your teaching experience at the beginning or end of each day. Reciting daily affirmations is another great way to reinforce a positive mindset. In your journey, you can find resilience and strength by choosing to remain positive and giving thanks in everything because this is God's will concerning you. When the temptation to seek alternative occupations arises, remember that true peace and contentment in life can only be found in aligning your life with God's purposes. Challenging days are a natural part of life in any profession. Let gratitude be the guiding light that transforms your teaching journey. It is in this state of thankfulness that you recognize that it is indeed a blessing and honor to be a part of this profession.

Abba,

I praise You that You are the God who created Heaven and Earth. I put my faith in Your Word which will not return to You void. I thank You for another day's journey. I submit my flesh to Your will for my life. I thank You for the good and the bad days in my classroom and my school. I thank You that You are the God who can cause everything to work together for my good. You are the God who gives beauty for ashes and an oil of joy for mourning. I surrender to Your will and Your assignment for my life. Forgive me for grumbling and complaining about my job. Thank You that the good days outweigh the bad days. Train my mind to see the good in every situation.

In Jesus' Name
Amen

Day 66 Guided by Faith

For we walk by faith, not by sight. 2 Corinthians 5:7

YOU MAY FIND YOUR JOURNEY as an educator unpredictable and filled with twists and turns. In those moments, allow these words from Second Corinthians to serve as a reminder that you are called to conduct your life not based on what you see with your physical eyes but on your trust in God. In moments when the future seems unclear, and the challenges insurmountable, let the light of your faith guide you. Embrace the uncertainty with confidence, knowing that your commitment to shaping young minds is part of a purposeful journey. Walking by faith and not by sight is walking in total dependence on God alone. Choose to speak the promises of God and not the problems that you see. Mrs. Melissa Godfrey's openness to implementing the "Number Talks" math strategy during the height of the COVID-19 pandemic serves as a great example of walking by faith. Faced with the unique challenge of teaching students concurrently, both virtually and in person, Mrs. Godfrey chose faith over fear. She could have surrendered to the difficulties of the task, however, her decision to incorporate the math strategy along with technological innovations elevated the learning experience for all students. Despite uncertainties, Mrs. Godfrey's positive attitude along with her unwavering faith resulted in significant academic gains and she became a model for other teachers facing similar challenges. Her story is a testament to the transformative power of faith in action. Like Mrs. Godfrey, let this semester be a testament to your faith where each step is guided by the assurance that all things are working for your good.

Abba,

Thank You that You are with me facing the challenges of each day. I thank You for Your Son, Jesus, and the gift of Your Holy Spirit. I take comfort in knowing that I am never alone in my classroom. You are right here with me and You have promised that You will never leave me or forsake me. Today, I walk by faith and not by what I see. Help me to learn to listen and hear Your still small voice within me, guiding me, and directing me each day. I thank You that nothing can separate me from Your love that is in Christ Jesus. I draw on Your strength to face another day and every challenge ahead of me.

In Jesus' Name
Amen

Day 67 Pay Attention

My son, attend to my words; Incline thine ear unto my sayings.
Let them not depart from thine eyes; Keep them in the midst of
thine heart. For they are life unto those that find them,
And health to all their flesh. Proverbs 4:20-22

BY NOW YOU ARE PERSONALLY familiar with the challenges of teaching a lesson only to find some students are inattentive or did not follow given instructions. In today's scripture, God encourages believers to attend to His Words, recognizing the human tendency, much like students, to forget or overlook instructions. In a profession where attention is paramount, prioritizing God's Word becomes an anchor. Jesus declared in Matthew 4:4, "Man shall not live by bread alone but by every word that proceeds out of the mouth of God." The message is clear that we should make a deliberate commitment to be a model student, paying close attention to Jesus' teachings. You can do this by setting aside dedicated time each day for reading and meditating on the Scriptures. Memorize key verses or passages that resonate with you. Engage in a local church or online Bible study group to fellowship and share insights with others. Stay open to the Holy Spirit's guidance and be receptive to continuous learning. As you immerse yourself in God's Word, strive to be a doer and not just a hearer of the Word. James 1:22 urges, "But be doers of the word, and not hearers only, deceiving yourselves." The power of God's Word is fully realized when it is actively applied. By attending to His Words, you will not only find a source of wisdom but also a foundation that will sustain you in your mission to inspire and guide the next generation. As the psalmist beautifully expressed, "Your word is a lamp to my feet and a light to my path" (Psalm 119:105 NKJV). In the journey of teaching, may you find comfort and direction in the illuminating power of God's Word, guiding your steps and bringing light to your professional and personal life.

Abba,

I praise You for Your Word. Thank You that Your Word is alive, active, and sharper than a two-edged sword. Give me a hunger and a thirst for Your Word. Help me to prioritize my life around Your Word. Your Word is a lamp unto my feet and a light unto my path. Just like I want my students to pay attention to my words because my words are beneficial to them. Help me to closely attend to Your Word. Your Word is health and healing to my body (Proverbs 4:20). I will hide it in my heart so that I might not sin against You. Heaven and Earth will pass away, but Your Word will remain.

In Jesus' Name
Amen

Day 68 *Every Need Supplied*

But my God shall supply all your need according to His riches in glory by Christ Jesus. Philippians 4:19

As a believer in Jesus Christ, you can stand on the promise of today's scripture. God, in His limitless love and abundance, is committed to meeting all your needs. This promise extends to every aspect of your life and includes your emotional, financial, physical, and spiritual needs. Approach this promise with solid faith, trusting that God knows your true needs and is fully capable of meeting them. This doesn't mean God will give you all your wants or desires. He knows what you truly need and promises to supply those needs. God is your Shepherd and He is more than capable of meeting all your needs according to His riches and glory in Christ Jesus. Instead of stressing over a perceived unmet need, spend time meditating on the goodness of God. Trust that at the right time, God will give you an answer or solution to every need. His ways are higher than your ways, and His plans often unfold in untraditional and unexpected ways. In the book of 1 Kings (17:4), God used a raven to feed the prophet Elijah. This unconventional means of provision serves as a reminder that God's methods are limitless, and He is not bound by our human understanding. Don't be surprised when God chooses to similarly meet your needs in ways that you don't expect. No matter what you are going through, let God know that you trust Him to take care of every need. He who did not spare His own Son, but gave Him up for us all—how will He not also, along with Him, graciously give us all things? Romans 8:32. As you navigate the various facets of your role as an educator, may Philippians 4:19 serve as a source of strength, peace, and hope. God's provision knows no bounds, and His faithfulness endures through every season.

Abba,

You are my Shepherd, and I shall not want. Thank You that You have always supplied every need in my life. I put my hope and my confidence in You assured that You will continue to meet every need. I trust that just like You take care of the birds in the air, that I am more valuable to You and You will take care of me. I confess that I need Your divine help and wisdom to be the teacher that You have called me to be. I cast my cares upon You and allow Your peace to settle my mind and my heart. I lift every student to You, and I ask You to use me to meet the needs in their lives.

In Jesus' Name
Amen

Day 69 Cling to Him

Draw near to God and He will draw near to you. James 4:8a (NKJV)

THINK ABOUT THAT ONE STUDENT who always clings to you. The one who wants to sit next to you and eagerly carry your things. You know, the one who is jealous of you and does not want to share you with classmates. They are excited to see you when they spot you in the grocery store or while shopping. This level of closeness and attachment is the kind of posture we should have towards God. Just as that student craves your undivided attention, imagine approaching God with a similar desire for intimacy. In prayer and worship, you can foster a relationship where you are excited to be in His presence. The Bible tells us that God is jealous for us and longs to have an intimate relationship (Exodus 34:14). When you humbly seek to know and serve Him, clinging to Him, you can experience the profound closeness of God. Imagine a scenario where your relationship with God is so impactful that it spills over into your everyday life. By drawing near to Him, you carry the influence of that relationship into every aspect of your teaching. When believers draw near to God, the promises of God become real in their lives. Peace, strength, hope, joy, and love will be modeled in your actions. This close relationship with God can have a transformative impact on your relationships with students, parents, and colleagues. Consider ways in which His love and wisdom can shape your teaching methods and interactions. According to today's scripture, when we draw near to God, clinging to Him, He reciprocates. Take the first step to draw near to God today, clinging to Him in a way you have never experienced before. He is a Rewarder of those who diligently seek Him.

Abba,

I come before Your throne today to acknowledge that You are the God of Heaven and Earth. I draw near to You today and I declare that there is none like You. No one can compare to You. You are The Author and The Finisher of my faith. I thank You for this day. Thank You for all of Your many blessings and Your goodness to me. I invite You into the details of my day as a teacher for Your Kingdom. Give me the wisdom I need to meet the needs of Your children. Thank You that You will never leave me or forsake me and that You are with me through each minute of the day. Thank you that You are jealous for me. Help me to draw to you like never before.

In Jesus' Name
Amen

Day 70 Fruit of the Spirit

But the fruit of the Spirit is love, joy, peace, longsuffering, kindness, goodness, faithfulness, gentleness, self-control. Against such things, there is no law. Galatians 5:22-23 (NKJV)

THIS PASSAGE BEAUTIFULLY SHARES THE characteristics displayed by a person walking in the Spirit. It highlights the transformative nature of yielding to the Holy Spirit and how this surrender demonstrates in the positive "fruit" of love, joy, patience, kindness, goodness, faithfulness, gentleness, and self-control. The fruit of the Spirit can serve as a guide for teachers to align actions, attitudes, and interactions with the principles outlined. To walk in the Spirit is to walk in victory over the carnal nature. The more you yield to the Holy Spirit on the inside of you, the more you will automatically display the fruit of the Spirit. One of my former students, Davinci, struggled with anger issues and problematic behaviors, making it difficult for both him and his classmates to have a conducive learning environment. After making numerous mistakes in my efforts to reach Davinci, I decided to approach him with a heart filled with love, patience, and gentleness. Instead of focusing on the negative behaviors, I took the time to understand the root cause of Davinci's challenges and offered a compassionate, empathetic approach. While writing this devotional, I unexpectedly bumped into Davinci's mother, who proudly shared that he would be graduating soon. This story underscores the importance of yielding to the Holy Spirit, allowing His power to infuse love into teaching through genuine care for students. This care extends beyond the classroom, fostering a compassionate and empathetic approach. Godly teachers not only impart subject matter but also instill values and principles of God's goodness, creating a lasting impact on their students' lives.

Abba,

You are the Bright and Morning Star. You are my Rock and my King. Forgive me for the days that I miss the mark. Thank You that if I am faithful to admit my sins, You are faithful to forgive. I come to submit myself to You and to resist the enemy. I declare that I am crucified with Christ, yet I live. It is not I but Christ who lives in me. Thank You that Your ways are not my ways, and Your thoughts are not my thoughts. Thank You for the promises in Your Word that You will never leave me or forsake me. Thank You that You are on my side, causing things to work together for my good. I choose to walk in obedience to Your Spirit. May the fruit of the Spirit be manifested in my life today.

In Jesus' Name
Amen

Day 71 Respect and Honor

Consequently, he who rebels against the authority is rebelling against what God has instituted, and those who do so will bring judgment on themselves. Romans 13:2-3 (NIV)

TODAY'S SCRIPTURE EMPHASIZES THE IMPORTANCE of praying for, respecting, and showing honor to our leaders, including those in our school environment. Avoid being quick to judge or criticize leaders, especially in a society where this behavior is a common practice. As a young teacher, becoming a school principal and district leader was never a part of my original plans. Although it may not be a part of your plans either, you could be a future team leader, principal, or superintendent of a school or district. Because you will reap what you have sown, I encourage you to honor your leaders and respect their authority. Give your leaders the same respect that you want from your students and parents. When questioning a leader's decision, consider that there might be additional details unknown to you as a teacher. As a principal, there was a time when I made a specific decision that sparked discontent among my teachers, including Sarah Jones. The school was changing, and many were skeptical about the reasons behind certain decisions. Instead of joining the voices of criticism, Sarah took the initiative to schedule a private meeting to discuss her concerns. In this meeting, she respectfully shared her concerns, seeking clarity and understanding. Appreciative of Sarah's approach, I explained the details behind the decision, shedding light on factors unknown to the staff. Sarah realized that the decision was not haphazard but was a strategic one. With this insight, she became an advocate for the decision within the staff, encouraging colleagues to trust the leadership. According to today's scripture, to rebel against authority is to rebel against what God has ordained. In essence, the scripture underscores the importance of giving leaders the benefit of the doubt and trusting in their decisions, even in times of disagreement, knowing that God ultimately ordains all authority.

Abba,

Thank You for the leaders in our city, state, and country. I want to also thank You for the leaders of my school. I pray for our team leaders, principal, and superintendent. I ask that You give them wisdom and direction as they lead our school. As our school board members make decisions, I pray that You will give them clarity and guidance. Give me the heart to honor the people who rule over me and to respect their authority. Help me to not focus my energy on their job but to focus my time on allowing You to mature and improve me. Take away the judgmental and critical spirit of leaders from me. Search my heart and know me. If there be any wicked way in me lead me on the path everlasting.

In Jesus' Name
Amen

Day 72 Setting Boundaries

Thou wilt shew me the path of life: In thy presence is fulness of joy; At thy right hand there are pleasures for evermore. Psalm 16:11.

AT THE END OF EACH day, do you find yourself mentally exhausted, replaying the day's events in your mind? Do you wake up thinking about the day and strategies to deal with a challenging student? Managing the mental and emotional impact of teaching can be challenging. To be successful in life, you must define clear boundaries between work and personal life. When the school day ends, make a conscious effort to mentally transition away from work-related thoughts. Instead of letting thoughts accumulate, you should intentionally schedule regular reflection time. View these stressful thoughts as your cue from the Holy Spirit to pray. This could be at the end of each school day or before bed. Taking the time to reflect on both positive and challenging experiences can help you process emotions and plan for improvement. Throughout my teaching journey, I utilized my commute home to pray and release negative emotions, providing me with a more positive mindset for my family. I have also found journaling to be very therapeutic. I encourage you to make self-care a priority in your routine. Whether it is exercise, hobbies, or simply relaxing activities, taking care of yourself spiritually, physically, and mentally is important. The Bible commands us to enter His gates with thanksgiving and into His courts with praise (Psalm 100:4). Spending time with God in quiet reflection and prayer will allow you to see challenges from His perspective. Today's scripture reminds us of the pleasures and joy that are found only in His presence. He will give you joy despite the many challenges you face each day. He will help you to enjoy your job and your career as an educator. Jesus came that we might have an abundant life which includes enjoying your life as a teacher.

Abba,

I praise You that You are the Omnipotent God. Thank You for the opportunity to commune with You. I bless Your name and I thank You for Your goodness to me. There is none like You in all the Earth. Thank You that You are bigger than any problem that I face today. I cast my cares upon You and I know that You care for me. Thank You for the joy and the pleasure of Your presence. Give me wisdom and ideas to deal with challenging students. As I commune with You, thank You that You strengthen me and equip me with everything I need to face all the challenges of the day. I trust that You are directing my path.

In Jesus' Name
Amen

Day 73 The Master Teacher

I will instruct thee and teach thee in the way thou shalt go; I will guide thee with mine eye. Psalm 32:8

IN THE HECTIC PACE OF a school day, teaching can often feel like a sink-or-swim profession, with vague instructions and limited professional development. The reality is that there will be moments when you are expected to complete tasks without clear guidance. However, as a believer, there's assurance from today's scripture that you have an ever-present help. The Lord will be your instructor and counselor. While training and coaching are valuable, the scripture emphasizes that God's guidance is ever-present. Jesus was a Master Teacher who used divine wisdom from the Father to explain deep spiritual truths using stories and parables to make concepts understandable. Jesus not only provided intellectual understanding but also inspired change in the hearts and lives of his followers. Beyond human instruction, God's wisdom can make a significant impact on your daily routine as well. Allowing God to instruct you is an invitation to acknowledge God's presence in lesson planning, classroom management, and interactions with students. Beyond learning conventional strategies from workshops and trainings, follow the example of Jesus by seeking wisdom from God and incorporating this divine guidance in your teaching approach. God's wisdom provides a timeless and insightful perspective that goes beyond the limitations of human understanding. Ultimately, today's message encourages a complete dependence on God for every aspect of your professional journey. He provides the best form of ongoing development, instruction, and support.

Abba,

Thank You for being I AM. You are my source and my guide. Your lovingkindness is better than life to me. I come to submit myself to Your divine hand. You know all and You see all. I come depending on You to teach me and lead me in the way I should go. I do not lean to my own understanding in the classroom, but I trust Your divine wisdom and guidance. Help me to not grumble and complain when things are not effectively communicated or expected of me. Thank You that You are The Master Teacher and I depend on You today. I trust that You can do what I cannot, and You have the answers to all my problems. Help me to hear Your promptings and obey Your Words. May Your will be done in my life.

In Jesus' Name
Amen

Day 74 Light of the World

Let your light shine before men, that they may see your good
works and glorify your Father which is in Heaven.
Matthew 5:16

PICTURE A LAMP PLACED ON a stand, brightening everything
around it. That -is you—called to be a light and an example for
Christ at your school. Your school needs the light of Christ in
you to shine brightly. How can you light up your school today?"
It could be a kind word, a helping hand, or a simple act of compassion. You can cultivate a culture of gratitude by expressing appreciation for your colleagues, students, and the school community. Listen actively, help when needed, and celebrate successes.
Be a positive influence in your school, like a light that brightens
a room. Do not engage in gossip or criticism; instead, focus on
praying and letting the kindness of Christ shine through your
actions. By doing this, you are not just talking the talk, but you
are walking the walk of Christ's teachings. And guess what? Others will see the goodness and, in doing so, give glory to God.
Reflecting on my journey, I transitioned from a successful tenure as an elementary school principal to a new challenge as a
middle school principal at Staley Middle School. Despite initial

reservations, I embraced the change as part of God's orchestrated plan. Ignoring the negative sentiments from coworkers, I saw the change not as a setback but as an opportunity to spread kindness in a fresh environment. Regardless of the circumstances that led you to your current teaching assignment, your encouraging presence is shaping the overall atmosphere of your school. Be a supportive presence for your colleagues and the school. Your light holds the power to make a lasting impact. Shine brightly and let God's glory illuminate every corner of your school.

Abba,

Thank You that Jesus is the way, the truth, and the life. Thank You that Jesus is the light in the darkness. I choose to plug into the source of light today. Show me how to let my light shine in my school and be an example for You on the Earth. I humble myself under Your mighty hand. I submit myself to the leaders of this school and this community. I surrender myself for Your use and Your purposes in my classroom and my school. Show me how to humbly serve others without complaining. Use my hands, my feet, and my mouth for Your service. Help me to have the mind of Christ and look for ways to serve, expecting nothing in return. You are my Rewarder and The Lifter of my head.

In Jesus' Name
Amen

Day 75 Time Management

Be very careful, then, how you live—not as unwise but as wise, making the most of every opportunity because the days are evil. Ephesians 5:15 (NIV)

TODAY'S SCRIPTURE REMINDS BELIEVERS TO approach life with wisdom, making the most of every opportunity. In education, time is a precious commodity, and time management is important for a classroom and a school to run efficiently. You must dismiss your class on time, take your class to lunch on time, rotate to the next group on time, etc. Most teachers use a timer to help make sure they stay on track for the day. However, effective time management is not just about running a tight ship. It's also about maintaining your sanity and finding that sweet work-life balance. According to scripture, you can maximize your time by prioritizing spending time with God to set the tone for each day. But seek ye first The Kingdom of God, and His righteousness; and all these things shall be added unto you (Matthew 6:33). Prioritizing your relationship with God sets the foundation for a day filled with peace and productivity. You can also maximize your time by dedicating planning periods for lesson preparation and avoiding unnecessary tasks during this valuable time. Remember to take advantage of grading apps and other educational software designed to streamline tasks and save time. Embrace the principle of "less is more" by focusing on impactful teaching methods rather than overwhelming yourself with unnecessary tasks. If possible, delegate administrative or non-teaching tasks to support staff. Ask God for more ways to protect your most valuable resource of time and how to make the most of every opportunity. Life's a journey so, pause, ask God for help, use time-saving methods, and let each day be meaningful and productive.

Abba,

This is the day that You have made, and I will rejoice and be glad in it. I come to confess that I am worn out and I need Your help. You have said in Your Word that I should be anxious for nothing. I come to surrender my will to You. I come to offer You my life. I am Yours. Apart from You, I can do nothing. I come to seek You first knowing that You have promised to add all these things to me. Thank You that You have not rewarded me as my sins deserve. Thank You that no matter what comes my way today, You have promised that You will never leave me or forsake me.

In Jesus' Name
Amen

Day 76 Empowered

I can do all things through Christ who strengthens me.
Philippians 4:13

WITH CHRIST AS YOUR SOURCE of strength, there are no limits to what you can achieve. Do not give way to thoughts of failure or think that you are inadequate for the job. Through the indwelling Holy Spirit, God has equipped you with everything you need for success. You are powerful in God and He promises that you can do all things through Christ who will strengthen you. In the insightful book *"Deliberate Optimism: Still Reclaiming the Joy in Education,"* authors Debbie Silver and Jack Berckemeyer declare that teachers have more power than they realize and should see themselves as visionaries and not as victims. These authors encourage teachers to pay attention to all successes, even the small ones, and to regularly reflect on achievements and growth. Take the time to celebrate success and be willing to take risks. When faced with opportunities that are outside of your comfort zone, such as leading a parent meeting or presenting a professional development session, resist the pull of fear. Instead, draw upon the strength of today's scripture that you can do all things through Christ. Take a moment to connect with God, exchange any fears for His confidence, and trust that His empowering presence will accompany you every step of the way. Allow God to calm your fears and declare His Word over your life. The same God who strengthened David against the giant stands with you. As you use this verse to overcome your fears, extend that strength to your students. Acknowledge their fears—fear of failure, fear of embarrassment—and create a classroom environment where they feel secure making mistakes and embracing their authentic selves.

Abba,

Thank You that You are the faithful God. Where You lead, I will follow. I will not fear because I know You are with me. Thank You that You are on my side and causing all things to work together for good. I embrace Your promise that if I draw near to You then You will draw near to me. You know the task that is ahead of me. Help me to stand boldly and confidently in You. I can do all things through Christ. I pray for every student in my classroom. You know what each of them is experiencing. I thank You that You have given me the victory in Christ Jesus. I receive and I enforce Your victory in my life.

In Jesus' Name
Amen

Day 77 The Command to Love

By this shall all men know that you are My disciples,
if Ye have love one to another. John 13:35

JESUS COMMANDED US TO LOVE one another. This love, however, is not contingent on feelings but is a deliberate choice. Loving the child displaying challenging behaviors or the irritating coworker requires intentional effort. The loving response to the student in your class who consistently disrupts the lesson or challenges your authority does not begin with an office referral. Attempt to understand the student's perspective, address their needs, and guide them with patience and empathy. In dealing with a challenging parent, communicate openly, listen actively, and strive to find solutions. You are called to let the love of God guide your actions and reactions toward others. Consider the story of Tyler, a student in my classroom who presented challenging behaviors. His disruptive actions, defiance of authority, and disregard for classroom rules tested my patience. Rather than reacting with frustration to Tyler's refusal to complete assignments and his off-task behaviors, I chose to respond with patience and empathy. Requiring Tyler to stay after school to complete unfinished work unveiled the root causes of his challenging behaviors—learning gaps that were masked by disruptive actions. Choosing to address these challenges with additional support rather than punishment transformed not only Tyler's behavior but also cultivated a positive and trusting relationship. This approach reflected the love of God and fostered positive change in Tyler's behavior. Choosing to model the love of Christ, even when it seems challenging, will set you apart from the world. Reflect on the love God demonstrated—He loved us even when we were sinners, offering undeserved grace and mercy. Seek God's help in extending the same grace and mercy to others, understanding that through your actions, people can witness the love of Christ in you.

Abba,

Thank You for this day. Thank You for the people that You have strategically placed in my life. Every child that sits in my classroom was divinely placed there by You. You have not made any mistakes concerning me. Help me to show love to those that are hard to love. Help me to show the same grace and mercy to others that You have shown me. I lift every student in my classroom to You. You know the root cause of their behaviors. Help me to see others the way You see them. May Your will be done in my life.

In Jesus' Name
Amen

Day 78 Faithful God

Faithful is he that calleth you, who also will do it.
1 Thessalonians 5:24

GOD IS FAITHFUL! FAITHFULNESS MEANS that He is 100% reliable and trustworthy. Take a moment to consider the instances this semester where God's faithfulness has been unmistakably evident. Reflect on the times He provided the wisdom needed for a challenging lesson, the strength required during demanding days, or the solutions to obstacles that seemed insurmountable. These moments are not mere coincidences; they are glimpses of God faithfully working in your life. You have a little more than ten days remaining in this semester, and you can rest assured that God will faithfully complete His work. Allow this biblical truth to impart peace and confidence in your heart. "Being confident of this very thing, that He who has begun a good work in You will complete it until the day of Jesus Christ." (Philippians 1:6). Despite the circumstances and difficulties you may be facing, keep your focus on God and not on the challenges you face. Trust that God will bring you to a successful end to this school year for His Glory. God never changes and He will always be consistent in His character. It is impossible for Him to call you and then not preserve you. No matter how difficult the days ahead may seem, declare your faith and trust in God to see you to the end. Verbalizing your trust in God's faithfulness can impact your mindset and foster a positive outlook needed for the remainder of the semester. His consistency provides a stable foundation for believers, even in the face of uncertainty. May the assurance of His faithfulness bring peace and confidence as you approach the end of this semester. Remember, He is with you through it all.

Abba,

I praise You because You are the same, today, yesterday, and forever. You have predestined me to teach Your children and to do Your will. You have begun a good work in me, and You are faithful to bring it to completion. I thank You in advance for a successful end to this school year. Thank You that You have given your angels charge over me to protect me in all my ways. I trust that You are with me, and You will never leave me or forsake me. I put my trust in You, and I lean not to my own understanding. Thank You that when I stand before my students You are with me. Thank You for Your faithfulness to me.

In Jesus' Name
Amen

Day 79 Freedom in Daily Decisions

There is therefore now no condemnation to them which are in Christ Jesus, who walk not after the flesh, but after the Spirit.
Romans 8:1

IT IS BELIEVED THAT TEACHERS make over 1,500 decisions per day. This means that decision-making is ongoing throughout the day with little or no time to analyze or reflect. There will be times when a parent may feel that you acted unprofessionally as it relates to their child, or your principal and school leaders may question your decisions. You should take time to reflect on your actions, but you must not condemn yourself for a decision that you made in good faith in a split second. Today's scripture is a reminder that there is no condemnation for those who walk in Christ Jesus. Whether in hindsight you feel the decision was right or wrong, you must remind yourself that you are not condemned. As a middle school science teacher, I recall my first interaction with an angry parent. The parent was upset because her son fell short of a passing grade on a progress report due to missing assignments. The parent explained that personal circumstances should have been considered and demanded that I reconsider the grade. Despite the pressure and parental scrutiny,

I stood by the grade but promised to work with the student for improvement before the report card. After speaking with my lead teacher and mentor, I learned options to implement for missing assignments. I acknowledged the decision was made in good faith and chose not to dwell on the decision but focused on the student's plan for improvement. In this profession, you cannot beat yourself up or second-guess your decision-making skills. Cut yourself some slack, hold your head up, and keep moving forward. Do not constantly rehearse past interactions. Keep short accounts with God. Give Him all the details of your day. According to today's scripture, God does not condemn you so you must not condemn yourself.

Abba,

I bless You for Your goodness to me. I come boldly to Your throne to receive grace in my time of need. Thank You for being with me at each decision of the day. Thank You for sending Your Son, Jesus to save and redeem us back to You. Thank You for not condemning me and for reminding me that I should not condemn myself. I choose to walk in forgiveness with others. Help me to not replay negative conversations and interactions with parents, students, and coworkers. Thank You that my light affliction is working for an exceeding and eternal weight of glory.

In Jesus' Name
Amen

Day 80 God is for You

What shall we then say to these things? If God be for us,
who can be against us? Romans 8:31

TAKE A MOMENT TO PAUSE and reflect on the power of God operating in your life. Romans 8:31 is a reminder that, as an educator, you are not alone in your endeavors. The God who holds the universe in His hands is intimately involved in your professional journey. The question "Who can be against us?" answers itself. If God is for us, of course, no one can be against us! God is the final authority and is in complete control. When you align yourself with God, no human authority can stand against His purpose for your life and career. A similar scripture, Isaiah 41:10 (NKJV), confirms this sentiment: "Fear not, for I am with you; be not dismayed, for I am your God; I will strengthen you, I will help you, I will uphold you with my righteous right hand." God's presence not only supports you but also strengthens and upholds you. Recognizing God's unwavering support allows you to step into each day with a profound sense of confidence and purpose. You are not alone on this educational journey. God stands with you, as a guiding presence that protects and empowers, making every interaction an opportunity to positively impact lives.

Reflect on this truth; let it be a wellspring of strength as you continue to fulfill your calling in education. If God is for you, no challenge, no obstacle, and no opposition can stand against you. Embrace this divine truth, draw strength from it, and let it be a source of encouragement as you mold the minds and hearts of the next generation.

Abba,

I praise You because You are the Most High God. You are my strong tower. Thank You that You are on my side and causing all things to work for good. I will not fear what people can do to me. I humble myself under Your mighty hand today. I thank You that You have given me the victory and will cause me to overcome the plots and plans of the enemy in my life. No weapon that is formed against me will prosper. You have given Your angels charge over me. I know that You will keep me in perfect peace as I keep my mind on You.

In Jesus' Name
Amen

Day 81 Teach with Equity

...God is no respecter of persons: but in every nation, he who feareth Him and worketh righteousness is accepted by Him.
Acts 10:34-35

IN THE EYES OF OUR Creator, there is no partiality. To please God, you must be extra careful to treat every child that He created as important. Teacher favoritism is giving special treatment to certain students. Be purposeful about not showing favoritism to students based on outward appearances. Many teachers unconsciously show favoritism to the children who dress nicely, have good hygiene, or are children of colleagues. God admonishes you to treat all students equally, regardless of their personalities or behavior. Naturally, there will be certain students who have pleasant personalities, who are obedient and follow directions, however, you must avoid the trap of favoritism or bias. God's standard is one of fairness and equity. To create a welcoming classroom environment, you must treat each student with the respect and consideration they deserve. It may take extra effort, but you must find something good even in your most challenging student. Your role is not only to impart knowledge but to instill a sense of belonging and acceptance in each student's heart. When possible, incorporate different cultural perspectives into your curriculum. Encourage collaboration among students from various backgrounds. This not only enriches the learning experience but also demonstrates an appreciation for the backgrounds of all students. Ensure that disciplinary measures are also fair and consistent. Avoid favoritism when addressing behavioral issues and approach each situation with an understanding of the unique circumstances. Because our God is no respecter of person, model His love in your classroom. When you make your classroom a reflection of His inclusive love, you will positively impact the life of each student you encounter.

Abba,

You are The Creator of us all. You are King of Kings and You are LORD of LORDS. Thank You that You are no respecter of persons. You expect us to show love to the poor and the orphans. You have made every student in my classroom, help me to treat them all with the love of Jesus. Show me if any children need a special word from me today. Forgive me for the times that I have shown favoritism due to student behavior or physical characteristics. Thank You that Your ways are not my ways, and Your thoughts are not my thoughts. I surrender myself completely to You today.

In Jesus' Name
Amen

Day 82 Support New Teachers

He saith unto Him, Yea, Lord; thou knowest that I love thee.
He saith unto Him, Feed my lambs. John 21:15

THIS SCRIPTURE IS A CONVERSATION between Jesus and Peter after Jesus' resurrection. Jesus reassures Peter of forgiveness and charges him with the task of "feeding His sheep." Like Peter, you have also been called to translate your faith into action. Jesus summons each believer to take up their cross and to "feed His sheep" daily. In the realm of education, this command also involves supporting and uplifting new teachers who often face numerous challenges. As each day is filled with an abundance of things to do, be intentional about supporting and mentoring new teachers. Mentorship is crucial, especially with the omission (in some cases) of the student-teaching process. Consider specific ways you can support newcomers by organizing regular mentoring sessions, creating a welcoming environment, and sharing resources to ease the transition into the profession. It is crucial to intentionally provide the support and guidance needed for success. Additionally, consider ways to address the specific challenges new teachers face, such as adapting to technology, handling diverse classrooms, or managing work-life balance. These tailored efforts demonstrate a commitment to the personal and professional growth of new educators. When building relationships with newcomers, make it a give-and-take relationship and be open to learning from them. New teachers often bring fresh perspectives and innovative approaches. By actively implementing such collaborative efforts, you contribute to a positive and supportive community, reflecting Jesus' call to love and uplift one another. Take joy in serving your new colleagues and collectively share in the joy that comes from making a positive impact on the profession.

Abba,

Thank You for this day. Thank You for choosing me to work with Your children. I accept my divine assignment. I know that You are causing everything to work for my good. Today I choose to focus my mind on You knowing that You will keep me in perfect peace. I pray for my coworkers, especially those new to the profession. Use me as an example to help them along the way. Just like Jesus poured into his disciples. Show me how to pour into and encourage those new to the profession. I pray for schools and leaders. May Your will be done in my life and in the lives of all educators who You have commissioned and will commission to work with Your children. May we continue to support and encourage each other.

In Jesus' Name
Amen.

Day 83 Sacrifice and Abundance

He spared not his own Son, but delivered Him up for us all; how shall He not with Him freely give us all things?"
Romans 8:32

TODAY'S SCRIPTURE SPEAKS DIRECTLY TO the heart of your calling as an educator on a personal and professional level. It emphasizes the depth of God's love and the incredible sacrifice made for humanity. You understand the investment of time, expertise, and care required to nurture the growth of your students, mirroring the sacrificial love demonstrated by God. Teachers embody this scripture by going beyond the curriculum, investing time in individual student needs, and fostering a positive learning environment. Just as God freely gave His Son, you freely give your time, encouragement, and support to your students. This also involves providing extra help to struggling students, offering words of affirmation, or being a compassionate listener to students facing challenges. Mary Hemphill in *"The One-Minute Meeting: Creating Student Stakeholders in Schools,"* encourages educators to embrace another vital sacrifice—engaging in one-minute meetings with students. According to Hemphill, this intentional strategy of having individual meetings with all students and asking simple questions like "How are you doing today?" or "What are you proud of this semester?" empowers students as active participants in the educational process. Making the sacrifice to provide students with a voice in the school improvement process can directly impact student achievement and the school culture. Continue to make daily sacrifices, guiding your students toward knowledge, growth, and the boundless possibilities that lie ahead. Take heart in knowing that these sacrifices are not in vain. The impact you make today has the potential to resonate far into the future, influencing generations to come.

Abba,

I praise You that there is none like You in all the Earth. Thank You that You freely gave Your Son to redeem humanity back to Yourself. I thank You for Jesus' sacrifice and obedience. Thank you that He made Himself of no reputation and took the form of a servant. I put my trust in You alone as my source and my strength today. I thank You that my future is bright. Thank You that You long to be gracious to me and to freely give me all things. I surrender myself to You today. I live my life for Your Glory. May your love for me be mirrored in my love for the students each day.

In Jesus' Name
Amen

Day 84 God Gives the Increase

So then neither is he who plants is anything, nor he who waters but God who gives the increase. 1 Corinthians 3:7

IT IS REWARDING TO WITNESS the growth of students from the beginning to the end of a school year. Students are like seeds, and you are chosen to nurture and cultivate these seeds. Every teacher before and after you water and cultivate the seeds. Think about your own life, there is no one person who you can attribute to teaching you everything you know. It was God using a network of influences along your journey. Ultimately, it is God who can take full credit for causing the increase. It is not important who the previous teachers of your students were because it is God who gives growth. Therefore, refrain from criticizing previous teachers for the growth or lack thereof in students. Similarly, do not take excessive pride in the progress observed in your students. All glory and praise belong to God. Kristen Anderson was by far one of the best math teachers I have had the pleasure to observe. Recognizing gaps in conceptual understanding among her sixth-grade math students, Kristen made a remarkable commitment. She volunteered to "loop up" with her students, extending her teaching journey to their seventh-grade year. By the end of the seventh grade, the students exhibited remarkable gains in academic achievement. Mrs. Anderson, displaying humility and a collaborative mindset, refused to singularly take credit for their success. Instead, she acknowledged the collective efforts of the entire seventh-grade team, including Mrs. West and Mrs. Garrard. In her dual role as both planter and waterer in the lives of her students, Kristen exemplified the collaborative spirit that contributes to positive outcomes. Her recognition of the contributions of her colleagues underscores the idea that individual teachers, working together, play vital roles in nurturing student growth. As one teacher plants and another one waters, it is God who brings about every positive outcome.

Abba,

You are the great and mighty God. There is none like You. You hold the world, and You are sustaining us. Like Jesus, help me to live for Your Glory. Give me humility as I plant and water in the lives of Your children. Help me to remember that it is You who cause growth and increase in their lives. I humble myself and take no glory for the great things that You are causing to happen in my classroom. I know that apart from You I can do nothing. It is You working in me for Your good pleasure. In You, I move, live, and have my being. May You get the glory for all the good things that happen in my life.

In Jesus' Name
Amen

Day 85 Answering the Call

Also I heard the voice of the Lord saying, Whom shall I send, and who will go for us? Then said I, Here am I; send me.
Isaiah 6:8

ISAIAH WAS WILLING TO ACCEPT the call of God for his life. Accepting God's call was no light task for Isaiah. He is referred to as the "weeping prophet" because he was called by God to deliver a message of judgment. The call of God on Isaiah's life came with ridicule and personal conflict. Choosing to remain in the education profession means accepting the call of God daily to be used for Kingdom purposes. Although you will not face the level of opposition that Isaiah faced, the call to teach does come with conflict and challenges. Accepting the call means denying the occasional desire to throw in the towel. The beautiful part is that God has promised never to leave or forsake you on the journey. During my tenure as an elementary school counselor, a remarkable story unfolded, one that highlighted the impact educators can have on the lives of students. Collaborating with Mrs. Annie Paschal, the counselor at the other elementary school in the district a special grant from the Department of Juvenile Justice called "Boyz to Men" was received. This initiative was specifically designed to provide crucial support for African American males in elementary school, offering them opportunities for training, mentorship, and engaging trips. Despite a plethora of challenges and the fact that we had never managed a grant, Mrs. Paschal and I were determined to serve this population of students. The program not only addressed a specific need but made a lasting impact on the boys served as well as the mentors in the program. You will not be exempt from challenges, by embracing the call of God daily, you become an agent of positive change in the lives of students. Continue answering the call, knowing that your influence is shaping the next generation.

Abba,

I praise You because You are the Mighty God. Today, I answer Your call and say yes to Your purposes for my life. I surrender my will to Your will. I take up the cross of educating Your children and I choose to follow You. I lose my life to find it knowing that a fulfilling life cannot be found apart from You. You are my Creator and You created me for Your divine purposes. I accept Your will for my life. I choose to surrender my life for Your greater purposes. I follow the path of Christ who humbled Himself and became obedient even to death on the cross. Use my life today for Your Glory.

In Jesus' Name
Amen

Day 86 The Blessing

"The Lord bless You and keep you; The Lord make His face shine upon you, and be gracious to you; The Lord lift His countenance upon you, And give you peace." Numbers 6:24-26

IN THE DEMANDING FIELD OF education, where you invest not just knowledge but also your heart and soul, assurances from today's scripture hold immeasurable value. It serves as a reinforcement that you are not alone on this journey. Your commitment to shaping young minds and fostering a positive learning environment does not go unnoticed. The assurance that the Lord sees your efforts and showers His blessings upon you is a testament to His faithfulness. The metaphor of God's face turning towards you signifies His ever-present and loving presence in your life. As you navigate throughout each day, may you sense the Lord's face turning toward you, a gesture of divine attention and care. In moments of weariness, may you find a peace that surpasses understanding knowing that He calls you by name. Allow His love to radiate in and through you and affect the people and the world around you. The world would be a dark place without the light of God shining in believers. You are an asset to your school and your presence is needed to fight the darkness of the world. Your current and future students need you to stay in faith and committed to the path that God has laid out for you. Let the scripture be a reminder that the Lord is with you, blessing you abundantly and granting lasting peace. This profound peace, grounded in God's grace, has a ripple effect, influencing not only your well-being but also the atmosphere in your classroom and the lives of your students.

Abba,

Thank You for Your beautiful presence. Thank You for the beauty of Jesus' sacrifice to redeem me back to You. May Your spirit fill me and may Your face shine upon me today. May I reflect Your light to others. I submit my will to Your will today. I come in alignment with Your plans and Your purposes for my life. I decrease and I allow Jesus to increase in me today. I pray for every student that I will encounter today. May they feel Your love through me and know that they are loved. Give me the wisdom and guidance to be an effective teacher for Your glory.

In Jesus' Name
Amen

Day 87 No Judgment

Judge not, and you shall not be judged. Condemn not, and you will not be condemned. Forgive and you shall be forgiven.
Luke 6:37

JESUS' WORDS IN TODAY'S SCRIPTURE are absolutely clear. You should not judge and condemn others. The standard you use in judging is the standard by which you will be judged. These words hold significant relevance in the realm of education, emphasizing the importance of understanding and compassion. In the classroom, where unique strengths and weaknesses are evident, the call to "judge not" encourages you to see each student through a lens of understanding. Recognize that behind every behavior, there may be untold struggles and stories. Your impartiality and openness pave the way for a compassionate and inclusive learning environment. As you manage student behaviors, strive to offer constructive guidance rather than passing harsh judgments. Your approach influences not only their academic journey but also their personal growth. Educators must be mindful of the spirit they convey to children. Students, like anyone else, can discern a spirit of criticism and self-righteousness. Many of the misbehaviors of students are a direct response to the perceived feelings of the adults in the school. In her TED Talk titled "Every Kid Needs a Champion," Rita Pearson (2013) emphasizes the importance of relationships in education. Pearson acclaims that, "Students do not learn from people that they don't like." They also don't learn from people they think don't like them. Educators must engage in self-reflection, examining their hearts and asking for guidance from above. Being judgmental and critical is pride, and as you know, God despises pride. Humbly ask God to search your heart and reveal anything that may not be pleasing to Him. Remember, He is the only Righteous Judge. As you journey to the end of the semester, carry with you the profound teachings of today's scripture. Let it guide your interactions, soften your responses, and infuse your classroom with a spirit of empathy, acceptance, and love.

Abba,

You are a great God and a great King above all gods. Thank You for a new day. Thank You for the people that You have placed in my life. Thank You that You have called me to serve them. Forgive me for standing in judgment of others when I don't have all the details of their lives. You alone are the Righteous Judge. You alone know all the details and all the circumstances of everyone's life. I ask You to search my heart and know my thoughts, and if there be any wicked way in me, lead me in the way everlasting. Help me to live a surrendered life that is pleasing to You.

In Jesus' Name
Amen

Day 88 Iron Sharpens Iron

As iron sharpens iron, so one person sharpens another.
Proverbs 27:17 (NIV)

HAVE YOU EVER HAD TO use dull scissors or a dull knife? These tools cannot achieve their purpose effectively while dull. Just like a knife, we tend to get dull as educators. Yes, you can get rusty and lose your edge through everyday use. So, how can you ensure that you stay sharp in the profession? Keeping with the analogy, a knife needs sharpening to reach its full potential, the same holds true for educators. Today's scripture is a reminder that, like blades, believers need others to sharpen them for effectiveness. It is common for teachers to feel frustrated and reluctant to participate in the sharpening process of professional learning and collaboration. However, this development is crucial to remain sharp in this profession. Participating in the learning process, whether it introduces new knowledge or not, is essential for maintaining your edge. Even if you do not learn something revolutionary, being part of the learning process allows you to continue networking and growing. While joining professional organizations, attending conferences, and seeking external professional development opportunities are valuable, there's also immense power in collaborating with fellow teachers. Do not underestimate the strength of a grade-level team. Working collaboratively with colleagues provides a supportive network that helps educators stay sharp and effective. Recognize that challenges will arise when people come together for a common goal. Work in a spirit of unity by being patient with others, forgiving others, and recognizing the common goal of imparting knowledge and fostering growth in students. We need others to polish and buff us so our effectiveness can expand. The power of the profession comes from working together. Continue learning and embrace teamwork for professional growth and success.

Abba,

I bless You for this is the day that You have made. I will rejoice and be glad in it. Thank You for reminding me that iron sharpens iron. Help me to be vulnerable with my fellow teachers and work to overcome offenses so that we can sharpen each other and support each other. I release my emotions to You, and I don't allow my emotions to lead or govern my life. I forgive the people around me for any offenses, and I walk in love. I allow You to use the people around me to sharpen me and develop me into the person You have called me to be.

In Jesus' Name
Amen

Day 89 Laughter is Good

A merry heart doeth good like medicine. Proverbs 17:22a

ISN'T IT WONDERFUL HOW GOD designed our bodies to experience laughter? When was the last time you had a good laugh? It is believed that laughter lowers the stress level and improves our mood and emotional state. The Bible says laughter is like medicine; it has a therapeutic effect on the body. Throughout the school day, there will be moments when students say or do something funny. There is nothing quite like listening to the joyful sounds from the playground during recess. Take the time to laugh with your students and coworkers. Laugh even when you make a mistake, it shows students that you are human, and mistakes are a part of life. As we approach the end of the semester, welcome the various activities that bring laughter and joy, such as the much-anticipated field days, award ceremonies, or enriching art programs. Field days present an opportunity for carefree enjoyment, breaking away from the confines of the classroom and textbooks. Award ceremonies acknowledge the hard work and dedication of both educators and students. Programs, whether artistic or academic, showcase the diverse talents and efforts of students, adding a vibrant touch to the end of the semester.

These moments not only provide a break from routine but also foster a positive and uplifting atmosphere. Do not allow external challenges to overshadow the joyous moments you can create and experience with your students. Finish the semester strong, knowing that your efforts are making a lasting difference in the lives of those you touch. As they say, laughter is truly good for the soul.

Abba,

I come praising You today because You are the Most High God. This is the day that You have made, and I will rejoice and be glad in it. Thank You for the gift of laughter and children. Thank You for the opportunity to work with young people each day. Thank You for their innocence and the joy that children bring. Thank You that You designed our bodies to laugh. Help me to slow down and enjoy the joyful moments of each day. Thank You for ordaining peace for me. I declare that I am more than a conqueror in Christ Jesus and You have given me the victory. I receive Your victory today.

In Jesus' Name
Amen

Day 90 Victory in Jesus

But thanks be to God, which giveth us the victory through our Lord Jesus Christ. I Corinthians 15:57

AS THE SEMESTER DRAWS TO a close, take a moment to reflect on the incredible journey you and your students have undertaken. Take the time to thank God for meeting every need and seeing you through each trial. He brought you through every mountain top and every valley experience of the semester. In my career, I had the privilege of working with Mrs. Volley who decided early during a challenging school season that it would be her first and last year teaching. Mrs. Volley, having transitioned to teaching as a second career, found herself as the third teacher assigned to the eighth-grade English class. She faced obstacles with learning the curriculum, classroom management, and implementing best practices. Despite the difficulties, Mrs. Volley determined that though she would be "one and done" but would still give her best each day. Unaware of the significant impact that she was having on her students and colleagues, Mrs. Volley worked late and on weekends to learn the curriculum, sought support from her colleagues, and planned engaging lessons for her students. By the end of the year, Mrs. Volley was shocked when her students showed significant growth on the state-mandated end-of-year assessment and several students selected her as their "Golden Apple Award" recipient. Students saw in Ms. Volley what she did not necessarily see in herself, a dedicated and inspiring teacher. As the school year concluded, she emerged not only as an exceptional teacher but as an inspiration for her entire school community. Her journey, much like yours, demonstrates that even in the face of challenges, there is victory, and through perseverance, you too can triumph. Today Mrs. Volley continues her journey as an amazing teacher. As you end this semester, end with the confidence of today's scripture, that He will not fail you and that He has assured you of victory this school year. Being confident of this, that He who began a good work in you will carry it on to completion until the day of Christ Jesus (Philippians 1:6).

Abba,

Thank You for being with me through each day of the first semester of this school year. I know that You will never leave me or forsake me. Thank You for causing me to triumph and giving me the victory for this semester of school. Thank You that I can do all things through You. I take the time to give You all the honor and glory for bringing me through this semester. Thank you for every child that you have given me the power to influence. I thank You for so loving the world that You gave us Your Son. Thank You for causing all things to work together for my good.

In Jesus' Name,
Amen

End of the Semester

Now unto Him who is able to do exceedingly and abundantly above all that we can ask or think, according to the power that worketh in us. Ephesians 3:20

WHETHER IT IS THE WINTER Break or Summer Break, the end-of-semester vacations stand as delightful rewards for educators. Amidst the constant hustle at school, of thinking, planning, and managing the energy of young minds, taking a break becomes essential. You have mastered so much including the art of a quick lunch and timed bathroom breaks. The semester break offers a precious opportunity to rejuvenate your body, mind, and soul. Make intentional plans to devote extended time to self-care and spiritual renewal during the break. Use this break to connect with your faith and let it replenish your mental and physical well-being. Prioritize saying no to commitments that could interfere with your much-needed time of rest, this includes saying no to teaching during extended learning opportunities. Allow yourself the luxury of uninterrupted sleep, free from the restraints of alarm clocks and to-do lists. Furthermore, cherish quality moments with your family, as this break provides a unique chance for undistracted, meaningful time together. Reading your journals (current and old) can be a valuable practice to reflect on the journey. Take pride in your accomplishments, celebrate the successes, and embrace the lessons learned. You are shaping the future, one lesson at a time, and your dedication is truly commendable. Thank you for all that you do. Enjoy this well-deserved break.

Abba,

I thank You that you are the same God today, yesterday, and forever. Thank You for Your faithfulness during this semester of school. Thank You for Your goodness to me. Your lovingkindness is better than life. I thank You for this much-needed break. Help me commit to spending extended time in Your presence over the break so You can refuel and recharge me. I don't want to get burnt out. I also thank You for every challenge and trial that You have allowed for my development. I give You all the glory for any success achieved this semester. Keep my students and their families safe over the break. Thank You being The Author and The Finisher of my faith.

In Jesus' Name
Amen

References and Resources

Berckemeyer, J., Silver, D. (2023). Deliberate Optimism: Still Reclaiming The Joy In Education (2nd Edition. Corwin.

Boogren, T. (2020). *180 Days of Self-Care for Busy Educators.* Solution Tree Press.

Hemphill, M. (2021). *The One Minute Meeting: Creating Student Stakeholders in Schools.* Cognella.

Jackson, R. (2018). *Never Work Harder than Your Students & Other Principles of Great Teaching* (2nd Edition). ASCD.

Linsin, M. (2016). *The Happy Teacher Habits: 11 Habits of the Happiest, Most Effective Teachers on Earth.* JME Publishing

Michael, M. (2022). *From Burnt Out to Fired Up: Reigniting Your Passion for Teaching.* Solution Tree Press.

Mielke, C. (2019). *The Burnout Cure: Learning to Love Teaching Again.* ASCD.

Pearson, R. [TED]. (2013, May 8). Every kid needs a champion [Video]. YouTube. https://www.youtube.com/watch?v=SFn-MTHhKdkw

Whitaker, T. (2012). *What Great Teachers Do Differently:17 Things that Matter Most.* Routledge

Wong, K, Wong. R. (2018). *The First Days of School: How to be An Effective Teacher* (5th Edition). Wong Publications.